The Story of a Migrant: a Personal Memoire

Donal Cruise O'Brien

All text and images Copyright © 2012 Rita Cruise O'Brien

First Printing 2012

ISBN 978-1-291-08082-7

Produced by Malcolm Woolliams at directionforward.com

TABLE OF CONTENTS

PREFACE	I
CHAPTER 1	**5**

Point of Departure: A Dublin Childhood

On the Edge of World Events	5
Early memories	10
Primary School	19
Move to Howth	23

CHAPTER 2	**27**

Family South and North

Family Memories	27
One Voice Only: My Grandfather	29
Howth Perspectives	42

CHAPTER 3	**47**

Apprenticeship in Migration: Boarding School

A Quaker Education	47
Newtown Incidents and Adventures	55
Thinking about England	61
Continental Horizons	67
Back Home in Ireland	69

CHAPTER 4	**75**

Swotting Around: A Student in Paris and Dublin

On my Bike in Paris	75

Trinity 87
Cambridge 94
London summer 96

CHAPTER 5   99

Taking Off: Cambridge and Africa
Cambridge: Tutorials, Rugby and New Friends 99
Africa: an Introduction 107
Conor and the Family in Crisis 111
Back in Cambridge 120
Africa: The Ghana Experience 123
Final Year in Cambridge 126

CHAPTER 6   131

Promised State: California in the Sixties
New Friends and New Ideas 131
Romance 138
A New Relationship and a New Family 142
Student Revolt and Setting up House 146
New Decisions 153
Marriage and Departure for London 155

CHAPTER 7   165

Quest for Knowledge: Research in London, Paris, Dakar and Touba
Research Ideas and new Academic Links 165
Settling into Life in London 170
Research in Paris 174
Arriving in Senegal 176
Research in Dakar and Touba 178
Dakar and the Completion of Fieldwork 190
Travels in Casamance 192
Leaving Senegal and Completing our Degrees in London 193

CHAPTER 8 — 197

Refining Ambition: London, Dakar, Algiers
    The Start of a Career — 197
    New Departures — 202
    The Onset of MS — 204
    Coming to Terms with MS — 206
    Advice to Conor: "Staying Alive in Ireland" — 212
    SOAS: the Institution as Hero — 217
    Research in Africa as Tourism — 225

CHAPTER 9 — 243

The Family, Academic Projects and Travels Abroad
    Maybe it's because I'm a Dubliner that I love London so — 243
    Ah les beaux jours! — 246
    The Franco-British Research Project — 250
    Gaddafi, the Tortoise — 253
    Academic Projects and Travels Abroad — 255
    Country Life in Dorset and Family Matters — 271
    Getting real: the need to divide up the spoils — 272

APPENDIX — 279

Stories for Sarah
    The Travels of Polo Bear — 280
    Wilber Whale and the Mystery Ship — 282

PREFACE

When Donal retired in June 2007 he spent a year reading widely and then began to consider what he would like to research and write. He felt that he had made his contribution to the study of Africa and wanted to think about Ireland. He thought of writing about Irish people living in Britain, considering how people felt in their adopted country, living through the troubles in the North from 1969 to the eventual achievement of peace. He contacted Irish scholars working in this area and was advised that what was sorely needed was autobiographical material. This suited Donal as he was a bit wary of undertaking a project which involved a great deal of interviewing because of the logistics.

He set about writing in Spring 2009 and it grew and grew into a substantial text. He seemed to enjoy his recollections and reflections of his personal story as a migrant. Several people among family and friends commented on the chapters as he went along, particularly Roy Foster and his sister, Fedelma Simms, with whom he shared so many personal memories.

By the summer of 2010 he had a substantial amount of the text in draft, but the severe downturn in his illness made it impossible to continue. He lay the text aside, which was a difficult decision, and began reading about the Irish Civil War, another great interest which lasted since his days at Cambridge. He was delighted to find that the historians who had worked on the subject since his school days had rethought some of the myths and misconceptions he always felt were taught to children and promoted to national significance.

Throughout 2011, Donal was in hospital continuously and in those very dark days little enough was thought about the unfinished manuscript. In July 2011, he met Mary Lynch, who was a nurse in the National Hospital and a kindred spirit. Mary is from rural Donegal and has always held Dublin intellectuals in some considerable circumspection.......until she met Donal. One day, out of the blue (when the text had remained untouched for more than a year), he asked me to bring in his chapters as there was someone who wanted to read them. And so Mary got him thinking again about what he had written in between heady conversations about Irish politics, the economy and the church together with a healthy exchange about the contrasts between country and urbane Ireland.

In the autumn of 2011 while Donal was still a patient in the National Hospital he dictated Chapters 7 and 8 to me and I brought them home for processing. John and Stephi Meyer from my family in Boston had given him a wonderful i Pad on which he could go over the texts on his own, and although a considerable technophobe, he greatly enjoyed the new acquisition.

Donal finally emerged from his long stay in hospital at the end of 2011 and we had six wonderful months at home with a great deal of care, nursing and medical attendance provided by the NHS. After a few months of enjoying our home by the river, reading poetry, listening to audio books and most importantly seeing friends and family who would drop in for lunch or tapas, we got back to work on in text. In May 2012 about six weeks before Donal died, he completed the final draft. We generally worked on it in the mornings when he felt up to it. He dictated and I sat at the computer. Suggestions flowed back and forth.

I have taken the liberty, following his death, of editing the entire text as Sarah had the excellent idea of private publication to distribute to all those attending his Memorial Service. Throughout the editing process, I laughed often at the stories I had forgotten. It has been a task of love.

During the summer I went through Donal's poetry books. He introduced me to poetry which was so strong in his family and national tradition. This was another glorious task. I found The Oxford Book of American Verse which I had inscribed to him on our engagement in the Spring of 1965 in Berkeley. In it I came across a poem which became my tribute to Donal with those few of us who gathered at his graveside. It remains my tribute to him.

Success
To laugh often and love much;
To win the respect of intelligent persons
And the affection of children;
To earn the approbation of honest critics
And to endure the betrayal of false friends;
To appreciate beauty;

To find the best in others;
To give of one's self;
To leave the world a little better,
Whether by a healthy child,
A garden patch
Or a redeemed social condition;
To have played and laughed with enthusiasm
And sung with exultation;
To know that even one life had breathed easier
Because you have lived -
This is to have succeeded.
Ralph Waldo Emerson,
American essayist and poet (1803-1882)

Rita Cruise O'Brien
London, August 2012

CHAPTER 1

Point of Departure: A Dublin Childhood

On the Edge of World Events

Born in Dublin on the Fourth of July in 1941, I have no memory of the war years: in neutral Ireland it was called The Emergency. I didn't even know there was a war or an emergency; there was no active part for me. My first recollection related to the war is of seeing newspaper photos of the sinking of the Japanese fleet - ships going down in ceremony: call it defeat or call it peace. I also saw the mains pipes laid out on the streets of Belfast, and the gas masks and helmets in my grandfather's house; just after the war had ended, the blitz had become a memory. I heard no bombs fall, no shots fired, saw no searchlights in the sky. But maybe I too could claim a tiny footnote to global conflict, "Donal and German Military Intelligence in Wartime Ireland."

My early life was affected by the backwash of the world war, in a manner which became a personal puzzle. My best friend for a number of years after the war was the son of a German military intelligence officer and his Irish republican wife - a slightly frightening figure. My friend told me with indignation that Ireland's so-called neutrality had meant nothing that the Free State had gone along with the British and it seemed to me that he had a point there. His father had something of a military bearing, but with sagging around the shoulders and the eyes. Looking back on it I would say that he had the appearance of a middle-aged university lecturer who wasn't expecting much in the way of promotion, Unlucky Jim. He was to do well enough in business, riding on post-war German recovery and the Marshall Plan. But add it all up; the personal outcome still wasn't great: so said the eyes, the shoulders, and the somewhat sad smile.

The mother of the family loomed large in their Sligo household, a property belonging to her father, an Irish Republican. She *was* a large person, taller and more bulky than her husband. She had dark hair, rather clumsy movements, and restlessness in the eyes, perhaps a little challenged. Germany's defeat must have taken her by surprise. That wasn't supposed to happen: "The Future (had) belonged to us." I don't think either of my parents had warm feelings towards her, but in 1940 Irish Republicans could still be forgiven their foreign policy eccentricities. After the war my father looked on her as a preposterous figure, disconnected from reality. My mother had a more pragmatic outlook: she felt she could be useful. I do also think that my mother took pride in the things that women/mothers organized for themselves, like child minding. But Christine didn't drop her guard and I don't think she ever really trusted her. She was haughty and impatient in the company of children, her manner making it clear that she knew things that she would never tell us, and we children would never know. She liked the expression, "You have to be cruel to be kind," delivered with a smile. She was kind to me, but her kindness to us children did have its worrying shadow. Her husband's sad smile also kept its secrets, but without his wife's claim to dominance.

The puzzle grew in my mind, towards the end of adolescence: why had my parents encouraged this friendship, pushed this friend in my direction? Neither Conor nor Christine was a friend of Nazi Germany, or of Irish Republicanism. It was no doubt convenient for my own parents to get me out of the house in the company of my young friend, roaming about Sligo or Dublin or (later) the heathland of the Hill of Howth. Not for me to wonder about any of this at the age of seven to ten, when I did find my friend a welcome companion.

The family grandfather was hardly visible to us children during long stays in his home in County Sligo. He was a real Republican, anti-British of course and pro-German too. I remember the respectful tones in the family discussions about Frank Ryan and of someone called Goertz, the latter having been a German spy in wartime Ireland who long escaped capture. Ryan was a Republican idealist who turned to Nazi Germany for political support. My own reaction to all of this was only to keep quiet, ears agog. I do recall an incident on the road in County Sligo when a group of children began to throw stones at my friend and myself, shouting "dirty Germans". I turned back towards them and shouted back something lame like that we were not dirty Germans: I was Irish and my friend, only German in part, but the stone-throwing did stop. He, who hadn't turned back or reacted to the taunts, told me afterwards that the stone-throwers were Protestants, by which I think he implied that they weren't really Irish themselves. I do also remember an occasion, at about that time, when my friend and I came upon a small Protestant church in our Sligo wanderings. He had a suspicious outlook on what might go on inside and he compared that church unfavourably with a Catholic church in Collooney, three miles away, a proper church with a steeple. Neither of my parents brought me to any church if they could avoid it, so it wasn't for me to comment: I still haven't gone to Collooney.

A few years later about 1953, wandering on Howth Head with my friend, we amused ourselves by throwing stones at the windows of what seemed to us (or we pretended to think) was an abandoned cottage, giving up when shouts came from nearby. My mother asked me about this a couple of days later, wondering if I knew anything about the two boys seen escaping up the hill from the cottage, a local landmark. I owned up on the spot, and my mother referred the case to the local policeman, Guard Loftus. The Guard seemed to be a bit surprised that I had volunteered a confession, and my friend was not at all pleased that I had confessed for him too. Why tell the truth? He never put the question so bluntly.

Another encounter, a few years on, brings us a little closer to world history. My father used his diplomatic influence, as an official of the Department of External Affairs, to get an invitation for my friend and myself to look over a Danish corvette on an official visit to Dublin Port. My friend's mother came along, and the three of us were ushered onto the ship and then off again almost immediately, it seemed to me, as soon as we had started ogling the guns. A long time later I asked my father what our precipitate exit from the ship had been all about. Conor told me that my friend's mother, who had not been invited on our trip, had come anyway and then gone to the ship's bridge and started a conversation with the captain. This included reminiscences of Copenhagen where she and her husband had stayed during the war. When the captain asked where she had stayed, the reply, "Gestapo Headquarters," got us all ordered off the ship, to my disappointment and perplexity.

Christine, near to her own death in 2004, told me that she and Conor in 1941 had been sure that they would both be interned in the event of a German victory, which had looked likely enough at least until the battle of Stalingrad (1942). So the deal was, that in the event of a German victory, my friend's mother would look after little Donal. I can see how this wartime pact could carry its emotional weight on into the post-war period. Neither Conor nor Christine had any brothers or sisters, and in a Nazi Ireland this family would have been as safe as any a guardian. But when told of what might have been, I renewed my debt of gratitude to Dwight Eisenhower, Joseph Stalin and, yes, to Winston Churchill and to all who fought for them, including the 150,000 volunteers from neutral Ireland serving in the British forces. One very small Dubliner had been on their side.

Early memories

While I don't remember much about the first four years of my life, two things about those years can be confidently supposed: that they were good times for me, and my mother. Maggie Kenny had very important roles in seeing to it that this was so. Maggie was sharp-featured in a mildly comical way, quick in movement and repartee, with a bantering charm. She ranked humanity in different colorations of stinker: the black stinker, a dismal category, accounted for most of us; while purple stinkers were her favourites, and she placed me there. I can't remember much of the rest of the rainbow, but those two colours endure. Maggie felt sorry for my family in its Godlessness, looking on my parents in a tolerant spirit, as errant children, unworldly, but not beyond salvation.

A hazy memory endures of the cries of approval for Donal's talking or walking, the signposts of growing up. My sister Fedelma was born in 1945, frail at first and remained very ill at an early age. My parents' anxiety was evident, as was their relief when the crisis passed; a holy glow around my little sister. My own contribution to the general good was to try to interest my sister in a radish. I remember: the very small shape in the cot, the blue eyes and dark hair. My mother suggested to me that softer foods were more in order. Fedelma may have looked frail, but she wasn't going to succumb to a radish.

Maggie and my mother made sure that we knew there was approval around. My first clear memory is of being shown (by my mother) photos of happy children playing at what was to be my first school: my reaction was to burst into tears. How could I have known in 1945, at the age of four, that those photos signalled the beginning of the end? There had been a Garden of Eden until then at 106 Pembroke Rd, Dublin.

Other early memories of our life at that address (in south-central Dublin) are of my mother cutting my hair while I looked out at the multi-coloured leaves on the trees outside and my disappointment that those colourful leaves had mostly gone by the time of the next haircut. I also remember all the stout bottles strewn around, the occasional half-empty glass, on what was no doubt a Sunday morning after a noisy party. Stale stout was no treat for the juvenile early riser.

As I write these lines, a painful thought comes to mind, about the happy laughter I overheard from those grown-up parties. There wasn't going to be much more of that kind of shared hilarity to reach my ears from now on; the secure conviviality of that gang was to be no more. My father was I think ascendant in that group, a star social performer and a gifted mimic: one party turn was as Adolf Hitler, burned cork moustache and histrionics in support. Tommy Woods, (diplomat and author of <u>John Stuart Mill and Poetry)</u> Conor's colleague and friend, sang the hopeful Nazi refrain, "<u>Und wir fahren, und wir fahren, und wir fahren gegen England</u>," and then roar with mocking laughter. Tommy's subversive humour, as well as his respectful conversation with small people, put him tops in my eyes. Paddy Lynch, later UCD Professor of Economics and Chairman of Aer Lingus, who went on long walks in the Dublin Mountains with Conor, was another pillar of that social group.

Things were however starting to go wrong between my parents, something I tried hard at the time not to recognize. Christine and Conor each maintained their friendships with the members of what had been their social group, on an individual basis; links which endured more with some individuals than others. My parents also tried hard not to let their discord be apparent to the children, while this child tried almost as hard not to believe what he was seeing, but all of that made for a tense enough family situations. It was Christine more than Conor who gave the hints, remarks about Conor's arrogance or his careless habits, while my father never said a critical word about her. I suppose one could see Conor's silence as a kind of eloquence, or as a register of pain, but over time I came to see it as heroic.

I can also remember my thrill at hearing and seeing the solitary night tram going past outside, with nobody at all about on the street, but the lights on in the tram, the driver and another person aboard, distant voices just audible from the tram. This would have been in 1946, checking the lines, just before the trams were to be phased out, replaced by buses like the number 18 which was to take me the mile and a half to Rathgar Junior School. But the night tram was my special memory. I slept in the front room of the flat, was the only one who knew about the tram, and I wasn't going to tell anybody else about it.

Maggie Kenny would sometimes take me out to a nearby canal path or to Herbert Park: I remember the canal lock; also the bandstand and the little lake in the park, both of which are still there. My mother took me once or twice to the beach at Sandymount, half a mile away: the sand on the beach was black as soon as you dug a spade into it, lots of rubbish strewn about. I didn't know how to swim, but if I had it would still have been an unenticing prospect.

On one occasion Maggie took me out to the house where she lived with her husband Mick and her father, in Kimmage, then an outer suburb. Her father, whose name I don't remember, had fought in the First World War. He showed me a very big book, including photos of the huge guns, accounts of brave Irish soldiers, but he didn't want to talk about any of that. Maggie's house was on an estate where she had been moved by the Dublin Corporation after the demolition of the inner city tenement where they had previously lived. I even think I can remember a glimpse of that tenement, where an internal brick had fallen, and the building been condemned. The walls in the Kimmage house were decorated with holy pictures, one of the Popes, another of a bleeding heart, strange stuff. On another occasion she took me, aged about six or seven, to the cinema, the pictures, to see a violent film about strike-breaking in the USA. It was some time before I could be persuaded into a cinema again, then to see Walt Disney's much more reassuring The Living Desert. My mother took me to the theatre, to see Hansel and Gretel, and I hid under the seat at the moment when they were going to push the wicked witch into the oven.

There were also outings to see pantomimes, but I didn't enjoy them much, too many grown-up jokes.

Other good company of my early childhood was Jeremy Craig, who was in the same class at Rathgar Junior School. Jeremy's mother, Joyce, was a friend of my mother's: the Craigs being our neighbours, exchanges of child-minding followed. Through the Craigs I was introduced to the BBC programme, "Listen with Mother," those posh voices. Joyce was kind but intense, an admirer of Gandhi. Her husband Victor was much more relaxed, with a warm laugh, easier company for this child. I didn't know it then, but Joyce and my father had been rivals as students in Trinity College Dublin, competing for the best scholarships. At kiddy's level Jeremy and I were also in our way competitors, for the top position in the spelling table pinned up weekly in our classroom. Rathgar Quakers didn't discourage the competitive spirit: the best spelling mark was coloured red. We sang of the "Bonny Bonny Banks of Loch Lomond", not of Irish beauty spots that I can remember. Another thing about the Rathgar Quakers was that they wore their pacifism lightly. I remember the enthusiasm with which we sang of "Marching through Georgia", Dublin bourgeois infants for General Sherman.

Conor was there all the time in spirit, no doubt part of the chorus of approval for those earliest mostly unremembered years. He told good stories, nobody read as well, in the evening after he came home from work. His career at the Department of External Affairs also gave me access to a prodigious stamp collection, so easily indeed that I soon lost

1. With Christine in Pembroke Road, Dublin

2. Donal and Grandfather Alec on the Dublin Docks, 1945

interest in postage stamps, but it also meant that he was away for the working day. In my primary school days I certainly looked up to my father, with love and respect rather than awe, and looked to him for a good story. When he came third in the parents' 100 yard sprint at my school's sports day, I was disappointed (no more than third?). I failed to see Conor's result for what it was, a magnificent achievement for the deskbound: his braces stretched as he pushed out his chest for the finish line. On the first occasion that I remember getting his sustained and undivided attention was during a bicycle ride (1948) in our neighbourhood. Crossing a curb, I fell from my bike, and then couldn't get back on, for my entire father's pep talk. In the end Conor did wheel me home, in a cloud of reproach, and then called the doctor.

Dr. Jacky Wallace ran his finger very gently down my shin and announced that I seemed to have broken my leg in two places. I was of course delighted: an important event with me at the centre, and took pleasure in the slightly critical way that the doctor looked at my father. It did hurt, but that's what I had been trying to tell Conor, and now it would be fixed. I would get off school, was promised a plaster cast to write on. Not only that, I was to get a bonanza of my father's attention, and such wonderful stories, as well as a huge siphon of lemonade. I think it was then that Conor read me Rider Haggard's <u>King Solomon's Mines</u>, the names of all those jewels; amethysts, opals, sapphires, wonderment. Conor liked to read to me a little ahead of my age, keeping the wonder going. And it was certainly at this time that I learned properly to read, all sorts of things to escape the boredom of immobility, including Kipling.

Conor liked to read out The Jungle Books, and I also liked to read them to myself.

I think it was at this time that Conor and I became good friends, certainly on a closer footing than before. He told me about Dr. Wallace's appearance in a Dublin court, witness for a jam company which had been sued by a customer on finding a maggot in the jam. Doctor Wallace pronounced the maggot to be the most nutritious part of the jam: case dismissed. So Jacky Wallace was a Dublin celebrity. There was also the reading to discuss. I could see that Conor wasn't too pleased with himself as far as our bike ride was concerned: maybe Christine had put in a word here? In any case the episode of the broken leg gave me a few points in the internal competition of family life: which is a happy phrase to introduce the birth of my sister Kate (Katherine Alexandra) in the same year. From a very early age Kate recognized that mischief might be her best recourse in dealing with two elder siblings. Her slightly crooked grin of pleasure when she had manoeuvred Fedelma or me into a difficult position with our parents is something neither of her elders was likely to forget.

We got our first car shortly afterwards, a black Ford Prefect that we called Griselda, and went for what was called "a spin", to the Dublin Mountains, the moorland of the Featherbed, with its views down over Dublin Bay. We had moved house by this time to another nearby flat, at 58 Upper Leeson Street, a ground floor flat with a difficult upstairs neighbour, Miss Murphy. My parents wouldn't speak to Miss Murphy, and didn't tell me why. So one afternoon, when on my own, I went upstairs and knocked on her door. She gave me a good welcome, lemonade and biscuits, and took out photographs and press cuttings of a train crash in central Europe (Czechoslovakia?). She had been in that train, and it looked an impressive wreck, up-ended carriages strewn about. A lot of the passengers had died in this crash: the carriages, which had been made of wood, splintered to pieces. Miss Murphy had been in the dining car at the time, which was the only carriage made of metal; it had held together and she had survived. I told this wonderful story to my parents when they got home, but while I don't think they were that impressed with the story of the train crash, they certainly were impressed that I had gone upstairs to talk to our impossible neighbour.

Primary School

My parents' choice of a Quaker school, Rathgar Junior, was explained to me at an early stage, emphasizing that Quakers (almost alone in Ireland) did not insist on religious instruction in school. Both Conor and Christine respected their moral values, particularly their tolerance. That was all a bit fine to me at the moment of first contact with the school; of being surrounded by a great many other people of my own age, a hubbub and clamour for attention. On the first day of school I made my own claim by noisy tears when my new satchel was snatched from me by an older boy, Richard Bewley, who made off with it up the school stairs. No doubt I had been showing it off, the bright shiny brown leather and the white stitching, and Richard had decided to put me in my place. Older boys did that kind of thing, and this episode did teach me the important lesson that in school you could not count on the approval you met at home. Thanks to a teacher I got my satchel back, all in due course, with a little pat and a reassuring smile. My clearest memory is of the noise and confusion, so many children about, so many satchels.

We were a multi-faith intake at school. There were Quakers, such as Richard Bewley, the aristocracy of Rathgar's pupils. There were Protestants, some Jews, at least one Hindu, and the children of intellectuals, like myself, who perhaps had no religion at all. Dardis Clarke was the son of the poet Austin Clarke and Jeremy Johnston the son of the playwright Dennis Johnston. Solly Ginwallah, Robert Leon, Zoltan Zynn were of our intake. Zoltan had a large hump on his back, a stoic expression on his face: he had apparently been the subject of Nazi medical experiment. Our teachers made the effort to make a clear distinction between Nazis and Germans, particularly as we were set to work producing (in my own case incompetently) knitted woollen squares to make blankets for destitute Germans.

Memories of my early years in primary school suggest that I must have spent a good deal of time looking out the window: the bacon rinds or half coconut hanging from the rail outside, and the birds that came to feed. Hyacinths were in small pots along the ledges (that great scent). There were also the nature walks: at Blackrock I collected in a jam jar what was pronounced to be a sea slug, an ugly enough creature and at Malahide we studied terns nesting and flying by the seashore. Of the classes not so much memory remains: geography (Miss Fennelly) was the best, to learn about faraway places like

Brazil. History had some good stories, the bad things that happened in Ireland for example, although our teacher did insist that the British were not our enemies now. The Irish language was not a class favourite in R.J.S. several of us didn't see much point in learning a language that nobody spoke. Our Irish teacher told us to get on with it: we would be required to pass national exams in Irish later on, in secondary school, so we'd do well to start learning now. Then there was mathematics, and that couldn't be blamed on the British, or on the Irish. There was, it is true, no religious instruction (in a separate class), certainly no indoctrination, but we did hear a fair amount about the sayings and doings of Jesus Christ. Moral precepts came with the stories, The Good Samaritan, The Expulsion of the Money-lenders, and The Sermon on the Mount. Perhaps all this came under the heading of General Knowledge.

Out-of-school activities included borrowing a book from the Carnegie Library in Ballsbridge, David in Baffinland (the fascination with faraway places). More time was spent reading the comics, Dandy and Beano for example: English comics featuring the schoolmaster's use of the cane on rebellious pupils (no cane, not even a smack, in the real world of my own school). In the late 1940s a new British comic appeared, The Eagle, reaching for more of a middle-class clientele, printed on better paper, in better colour. The lead story was "Dan Dare" and space exploration; square-jawed Dan had to confront aliens such as the Mekon, who took his wicked schemes about on his own miniature flying saucer. The Mekon had a huge head, not much of a body, and some in our school saw a parallel right before their eyes. My nickname was Mekon.

That did hurt, but the victim was neither helpless nor innocent. One of the first things I had done in school, having recovered from the satchel episode, was to carve the name of my classmate Robert Leon onto his own desk, which was next to mine. Robert had some trouble convincing the teachers that the carving was not his own work, and he was kind enough not to point an accusing finger at his neighbour. Looking back on that piece of nastiness now, I suppose I could try to take refuge in generalities: saying school is where we learn to torment each other, to prey on each other's insecurities. Jeremy Johnston read the fortunes of the pupils on their palms. When he came to mine he frowned, and then declined to tell me what he had read. Jeremy was a bit of a show-off in school, and so was I: he had scored his point. My outstanding achievements were to come in first in the high jump, with Dardis Clarke, 3' 6", and to write an essay on beavers in Canada that the teachers liked. Miss Fennelly and Miss Masterson talked to me about the essay, and felt that it pointed to a promising future for me: their hushed tones as well as their respectful words were my send-off from Rathgar Junior School.

A good school it had been, with teachers who enjoyed their work; R.J.S. sent you forth with as much of a good grounding as could be expected. Yet some of the most lasting lessons came from beyond the classroom, from family discussions and experiences out of school. There was one school-related horror to remember: Sylvia Gibbs, a fellow-pupil, had drowned when out with her family at Sutton Strand, next to Howth Harbour. She had been wearing water-wings, got caught by an off-shore wind and blown out to sea. Her father too had drowned, swimming out to try to save her. I didn't know Sylvia well, but she had a good smile, and Sutton Strand was a place I saw every day, going to and from school, the happy people swimming and playing. On another occasion, travelling on a bus in town with my grandfather, I saw a young lad fall down the steps of the bus and out onto the street. The bus had been moving fast: we did pull up; some people got out, and there was murmuring as to what had happened to the young man. He had been carrying two plates, one on each hand, no doubt delivering lunch to somebody, and had nothing to hang on to when he lost his balance. I think they were murmuring that he might have died; he would probably in any case have been seriously injured, another reminder of the precariousness of life.

Move to Howth

In 1950 we moved ten miles from the centre of Dublin to what had been the Bayview Tea Rooms, on the summit of Howth Head, the promontory at the north end of Dublin Bay. Thirsty would-be customers came knocking at our door, or window, for a while thereafter. The views extended 30 miles south down the East coast of Ireland. There was to be good swimming if you climbed down to Whitewater Cove, no sand but deep water, with nobody but yourselves about. Christine led the family group, with Fedelma and Kate and me, sometimes Conor too. Fedelma lasted longest in the cold water, and she came out coloured blue. I was also a competent swimmer by this time, having gone for lessons at the Blackrock Baths (in South Dublin).

For one year I was to commute into town to school, rising early to get the tram down the hill to Howth railway station, then into town on the train, a short walk from Amiens Street Station to O'Connell Street to take the number 15 bus to Rathgar. Count the return journey as well, that's quite a lot of daily travelling for a ten year old: so it seemed to me, and I still had to get back home by six in time to hear "Dick Barton, Special Agent" on the BBC. If I was late Christine was to listen and tell me, but try as she might she found it hard to take the story seriously: her quizzical expression survives.

There were rewards for the early riser on Howth Summit: first up and gone before anyone else had risen, you could take the cream from the top of the milk bottles for your porridge, with brown sugar a very good way to start the day. My parents never complained that the top of the milk had gone from all the bottles by the time that they got up. Christine did draw the line, however, when I started getting Mars bars on credit from the local grocery store on my way home from school. Of the journey to school, I remember an occasion when the train driver let me ride in his cab, against the rules as it was. There were other occasions when I saw barefoot children near to Amiens Street Station, the first I had seen of inner-city poverty. Nothing like that was to be seen in the middle-class neighbourhoods of South Dublin where we had lived. I was to leave Rathgar Junior School with a little more sense of Dublin as a city, just as I was about to depart from the city to travel

100 miles south to boarding school at Newtown School, Waterford.

The first ten years of my life thus were spent in Dublin, formative years certainly but still not enough for me to develop a firm identity as a Dubliner: no football teams, no treasured sites, and I wasn't anything like street-wise. Although I was clear in my mind about an Irish identity, thrilled to the sound of the national anthem, what about the names of the streets in the neighbourhood of South Central Dublin of my first nine years? Clyde Road, Waterloo Road, Wellington Road, and Raglan Road: these were glory names of British imperial history. The Royal Dublin Society was the centre of social life in Ballsbridge, a quarter mile down the road from where we lived: my mother took me to the horse show at the R.D.S. more than once. Those street names hadn't been changed after the independence of the Irish Free State in 1922 (they still haven't been changed in the Republic of Ireland today). Was I being conditioned to become what some people in Ireland derisively termed a West Brit? Maybe so, but then most people in that neighbourhood did not migrate to England. There were also the steamers to be seen from the top of Howth Hill, frequent daily traffic back and forth to Liverpool and to Holyhead. The British and Irish Line boats to Liverpool, with their hulls painted dark green and superstructures, pale yellow, went past Howth lighthouse, just down the hill from our home. A treat of the evening was to watch that boat go past while we had our evening meal. I didn't at the time (1950-51) have any ambition to be on such a boat, if anything I thought of Irish emigrants as lost people, but, again, maybe that evening sight did plant an idea at some level in my mind.

CHAPTER 2

Family South and North

Family Memories

My mother Christine was at the centre of my life gave me that core of emotional approval, and she reigned in my Garden of Eden, Pembroke Road. I can remember asking her the name of a large flower in the back garden, being told it was a peony, and seeing that it pleased my mother for me to take an interest in the plants. The garden was to remain a point of contact between my mother and myself. She planted a row of red roses, called Frensham, at our new home in Howth. I recalled the name of those roses to my mother during her short final illness, to her pleasure. Another point of contact was an interest in music, the sorts of music I liked, important as an axis since my father was tone deaf and indifferent to any music. There was a song, with the refrain, "Get out of here with your boom-boom-boom and don't come back no more." Christine explained that a boom-boom-boom could be whatever you imagined. Another link was an interest in sport. My mother had played hockey for Ulster schools (on the wing), and her father Alec Foster had been a very distinguished sportsman, centre three-quarter and captain of Ireland at rugby: he had also played rugby for the British Lions (in South Africa in 1903). I was encouraged to be physically active, not to neglect the sport and to keep fit. My mother kept herself fit all her life. She was also beautiful and very stylish, enough to give any little boy an Oedipus complex: brown hair and well spaced brown eyes, a lovely oval face, lithe in figure, with an infectious laugh. There was no hope for me to be a sporting star like my grandfather, but I did learn an important life lesson from my mother, which has served me well until now, to keep myself in the best physical shape possible. Christine's message did come with an edge, to be made sharper as time went on: don't overdo the intellectual side of your life, as your father has done.

I can remember visits to my grandfather Alec in Belfast, 27 Rugby Rd, from 1945 onwards, the first when his wife Annie was dying of cancer in an upstairs room. I was never allowed to see her. Annie Lynd Foster was the sister of the essayist Robert Lynd, who had left Belfast for a successful career in England, a writer with the New Statesman who described himself as an "escaped Presbyterian". Two of Annie's sisters had made their own escape, southwards to Dublin, where Dolly Lynd was a civil servant in the Free State's Department of Industry and Commerce, Lucy, a schoolteacher. There were many good Sunday lunches for our family with these two great-aunts, who lived in a flat on Rathgar Road, near enough for us to go on foot or by bicycle (until we moved out to Howth). Roast lamb with mint sauce was a favourite, and I paid nature's penalty once for eating too much of the sherry trifle with whipped cream.

Dolly and Lucy Lynd were a pair of chain-smokers who rolled their own cigarettes when not puffing away. They had brought their Northern accents with them to Dublin, as well as their passion for golf. Dolly didn't have a lot to say, although her manner was always welcoming: I'm sure she was very good at her numbers and also incorruptible. It was Lucy, the teacher, who did most of the talking, punctuated by wheezy laughter. And she made a point of talking to children, asking me about school experiences. She told a story of her time as an examiner when she had read what seemed a very good essay, featuring a train disappearing into a tunnel, leaving a puff of smoke as it went. Top marks, but then the next script's essay featured the same puff of smoke, and so on down the pile of scripts to be examined. A good laugh then and a shake of the head: Lucy enjoyed tales of misbehaviour. She and her sister shared enlightenment values: a large Michelangelo reproduction, the creation of man from the Sistine Chapel, dominated the principal room in the flat. The authority of age and experience at this address was never grim. Lucy kept up with what was going on: she told me in the 1950s, with a shake of the head, that "in fifty years' time nobody will have heard of Elvis Presley." Her ghost would shrug that off now, with another shake of the head, even great-aunts can't always be right. If ghosts can laugh, a wheezy one would also be there.

One Voice Only: My Grandfather

My grandfather Alec Foster was mostly bald by the time I knew him, with some silver hair, deep blue eyes, and an athlete's brown skin. While he wasn't of more than medium height, the build was trim and the step had a bounce: one could imagine what might have been his acceleration on a rugby field. He loved to walk, and I, to walk with him. There was one occasion, leaving the Dublin docks where we had been out for the day, when I made him a present of the crusts from the sandwiches that Christine had given us for our lunch. I had the nerve to tell him that he'd been a good grandpa to me, having myself eaten the best part of our lunch. His beautiful smile, as he looked away from me out the bus window, made up for any words.

Alec also loved to read aloud, or to sing when in the right mood: in the wrong mood he could turn to angry shouting. Alec's mood swings had been familiar to all who knew him, a preoccupation to my mother who had been his pupil in secondary school. Christine taught me to be wary with Alec, to be aware that there was a problem of mental stability. He had been in hospital and diagnosed as manic-depressive. Most of the time that I was to know him the poor man was toward the depressive end of that cycle. At the other end he was more fun, but also more of a problem to those who cared for him. In mania he was a problem, but he could be magnificent.

There was some political instruction too for me in keeping company with my grandfather, not that Alec could have been bothered with such a subject: no lectures, certainly, but songs and stories as well as many little hints, material for me to set about the formation of a messy national identity. Alec was proud to be Irish, to have worn the rugby captain's green jersey, but he was also proud to have played for the British Lions: no problem in rugby, being Irish and British too. He was also a Derry patriot who looked back with fascination to St. Columba, the aristocratic Irish monk of the seventh century who had set sail from Derry to found the monastic settlement of Iona, bringing Christianity to the heathen Scots. Alec sailed in a yacht from Derry to Iona with my mother Christine, replicating Columba's voyage: she remembered swimming with him in a cave.

My grandfather was Headmaster of Belfast Royal Academy, a leading secondary school where he also taught Latin and Greek. The Academy was co-educational, had been founded in a spirit of enlightenment and tolerance in 1785. In a history of the Academy, Alec, was said to have been influenced by the Gaelic League and introduced Irish history in addition to English history as a subject in the Academy. The pupils also learned Irish folk dances and songs, which was unusual in a Protestant school. There was no religious instruction, but at morning roll call there was a prayer and a reading from the Bible, during which pupils stood according to Presbyterian custom. Two Catholic teachers and some Jewish pupils waited outside in the hall, and only came in for the notices, thus demonstrating respect for other creeds. These were very much the procedures adopted in Quaker-managed schools south of the border.

The Academy's enlightenment values were combined with an element of Irish cultural nationalism. A friend of my grandfather told him, while they were playing golf on Cave Hill, that one of the Academy's Catholic teachers was "chief of the O'Donnell clan". The headmaster was very pleased about this and said that in singing classes in future the battle hymn of the clan, "O'Donnell Abu!" should be practiced. Soon afterwards this wild music rang out over the respectable

Presbyterian district and shook the windows. Often the methods and aims of the headmaster led to rows with the Board. That does sound like my grandfather.

Alec Foster loved the stories of ancient Greece and Rome, as well as all sorts of other songs and stories. The 19th-century British historian Macaulay, Protestant and romantic, with a poetic touch, was read to us in the evening, from the ballad of brave Horatio in ancient Rome to the account of the lifting of the siege of Derry in 17th century Ireland. The Protestants were the liberated heroes in Derry, from what one could call a Catholic siege, and Alec clearly enjoyed the account of their liberation. He also rather shamefacedly enjoyed the swagger of the Orange Protestant 12th of July parades in Belfast, walking along with a swagger of his own while assuring us that there was "terrible bigotry in those songs."

Songs and stories Alec would deliver with gusto. I remember his command of the family dining table, his demand for recognition of "one voice only" - his own. But fun was never far away at this time (1950s) when he was around. I remember an occasion, travelling with him on the train from Belfast to Dublin when he got me into the guard's van to ride on the back of a giant tortoise (in transit between zoos). He often took me on long walks. The centre of Belfast, with all the flags on display; the Protestant Shankill Road right next to Catholic Falls Road, flags which looked strange to this little Dubliner. I do also remember an occasion when Alec's parents came to Rugby Road (about 1946) for a family photograph with my parents. Alec's parents seemed a stiff old pair, not much of a smile to be seen, but the revelation to me was to see the way that Alec behaved in their company, fussing nervously. To see a grandfather behaving like a boy was a moment never to be forgotten by a grandson. .

I didn't know it then, but Alec at the time did have good reason to be nervous. Not only had his daughter gone and married what was taken in the North to be a Catholic, my agnostic father, he was doing something even worse himself by marrying Betty Guidera, a Catholic from Tipperary who had cared for his dying Annie. Even worse than that was soon to come, Alec was to declare himself a Catholic. In Ulster the Protestants have a song about this kind of situation: "The Ould Orange Flute." The song's anti-hero, a Protestant weaver and flautist from County Tyrone called Bob Williamson, "marries a papist called Bridget McGinn". Bob had played the flute for the Orange Order, "and all of us thought him a stout Orange blade." He proved himself to be "a deceiver", however, and by marrying a Catholic, Bob "forsook the old cause, that gave us our freedom, religion, and laws." Fallen among Catholics, the flute is "sentenced and burned at the stake as heretic....But as the flames roared around it, they heard a strange noise, 'twas the ould flute still playing 'The Protestant Boys'."

That song is the story of what happened to my grandfather. At one level "The Ould Orange Flute" is a cosy Protestant joke, for smiles among friends, but at another level it is a tribal warning. When "Bob Williamson's" marriage to a Catholic and conversion to Catholicism become known, "the boys of the town made some comment upon it, and Bob had to flee to the

Province of Connaught." Alec had never been close to the Orange Order; throughout his life was an opponent of what he saw as Protestant bigotry. But a Protestant and Presbyterian he had been, even if a Catholic he had now become, and now he was to suffer social exclusion, not the roughneck procedures implicit in the song. The roughnecks in the song were small-town boys. Alec was to get the big city middle class version, cold, respectable exclusion, closed doors and unanswered calls. Rugby hero though he was, pillar of society though he had been, Alec was to be shunned by most of the people whom he had known all his life. My mother never forgave the closed doors for Alec in Belfast: many years later I had the impertinence to remark to Christine that the Protestant Unionists of the North were "your people", and she had simply replied that she hadn't considered them her people since they had turned their backs on Alec.

While I didn't see Alec's exclusion directly, I heard an echo in a discussion among his Belfast family and friends, when there was mention of someone who had "married a Catholic." Something about the tone of voice, but, ever the little upstart, I put them the rhetorical question, "What's wrong with marrying a Catholic? My mother married a Catholic." A long silence followed. I also remember being perplexed by the assurance with which these formidable elderly Belfast Protestants could tell that someone was a Catholic. I asked one of them, "How can you tell?" The answer was immediate: "You can always tell a Catholic by the shifty look in the eyes". My informant would have known that I was some sort of Catholic myself, so the information was delivered as a deliberate rebuke. And I don't think I had a shifty look in the eyes.

At Alec's home, there was the children's life of the lane behind Rugby Road, my playmates Rex Berrington and Egan Crowley. Rex and Egan and I prepared ourselves for the dreaded visit of one Galway, who apparently had vowed to come and "get" us. Galway never did come, at least when I was around, but he worked well as a nightmare to bond our little group. We were working on a barricade. Belfast had been an unusual kind of place: for one thing there was rationing, which seemed to be very good news for children. There were no sweets rations (or any other rations) in Dublin. So we all enjoyed the wartime sweets.

Alec and Betty's wedding in County Tipperary was another part of my education in the ways of family and religion in Ireland. Betty Guidera's father, a red-faced farmer, welcomed Alec into the family, and Alec returned the welcome with his own attempt at geniality. It didn't sound right to me, and I could see unease in the audience. Betty was a lot younger than my grandfather, younger than Christine, and there may have been some disapproval on those grounds to complicate the inter-faith issue. Betty was of medium height, with a pretty face and a good figure: dark hair, brown eyes, and an occasional cheeky grin. When Maggie Kenny heard of the proposed marriage, she had called Alec a "dirty devil," albeit with a giggle, words for which my mother never forgave her, perhaps because she had been thinking something similar herself.

A short while after their marriage, Alec bought a cottage in County Donegal, in Fanad on Loch Swilly, a tiny house on a beautiful site, just up the hill from a mile-long beach, itself part of a twenty mile inlet from the Atlantic. For a time, they maintained their principal residence in Belfast. I spent a summer holiday in Fanad in 1947, when the sun never set. Memories remain of a long walk with Alec up over the hill from his house to Knockalla Fort, a ruin overlooking the Swilly; of Alec beating down the ferns, which were well above my head, to clear us a way.

The first time that we arrive in Fanad, we came by rail to Letterkenny, at the foot of Loch Swilly, that long Atlantic inlet, and at the station we took a " pony and trap" for the rest of the journey. I was a bit disappointed the next year when, instead of the pony and trap, there was a large American car at Letterkenny Station, a taxi to take us to Fanad: maybe a bit more comfortable, and certainly quicker, but to a small boy from town, much less exciting. Once we got to the cottage I got down to business with a friend who had come from Dublin with us building a dam in the little stream that ran in front of the cottage. However well we built the dam, with twigs and branches and clods of earth, it always leaked, although it did better service than another dam which we built on the beach itself, where the stream ran out to sea. So we learned something: you can't build a dam with sand alone, and we turned our construction interests to sand castles. My sister Fedelma remembers a friend helping us out with the turret of the castle, putting his lighted cigarette at the top to give us a realistic puff of smoke. I went back to Fanad thirty years later. Alec's cottage is still there, but no dam anywhere to be seen. The stream still runs out more or less at the same place across the beach to the sea.

When we got fed up with building dams or sand castles, there remained lots of opportunities for further exploration. At the far end of the long beach was a crashed aeroplane, a Douglas DC 3 (we boys knew that much of our planes) doubtless a wartime relic. Alec and Betty, meaning mostly Betty, looked after us, sometimes Christine and more rarely Conor were around. But it was a small cottage, room for a few children not too many adults: for all of us during the day, most enticingly in favourable weather, there was plenty of room on the beach or in the hills behind. With my friend, we spent most of the day on the beach, swimming or sunbathing. It was also a good place to ride bicycles and fall safely. There was one occasion in particular when we were at a pool up from the beach, near the cottage, watching a newt with its lizard-like tail and its tiny feet. Behind us appeared a local man, Dan Logan, asking if we had seen any fish. He ignored our negative answer, and stooped down, bending his knees, dropped his hand in the stream with an air of intense concentration. After about thirty seconds, he stood up in satisfaction. All I saw of the trout was a brown blur of speckles, and then its tail disappearing into Logan's brown canvas shoulder bag, as away he went without another word.

In the evening there were Alec's songs and stories: one song in particular, about a ship-wreck long ago in the bay before us,

3. With great grandparents in Belfast

4. Christine, Alec, Kate and the family dog at Whitewater

5. With sisters, Kate and Fedelma, and a friend at Whitewater

6. The View from Whitewater

was to come back again and again. The Saldanha, sailing out from the naval base at Rathmullen, at night against a very stiff wind - Nor-Nor West - had struck Swilly rock, under the sea at the far side of the bay, and sunk with the loss of everybody aboard. One of the crew swam as far as our beach, but "died upon the strand." Alec's treasure was the brandy cask of the captain of the Saldanha, Sir William Pakenham I thought that there was a hint of local knavery in the way that Alec told his story. Perhaps the ship had been lured to the rock. "Beware the Magherawarden Beagles." Perhaps a light had been deliberately pushed out of place. My sister Fedelma, who also heard her share of the Saldanha song and story, told me not to be silly. The Saldanha was a naval ship; there'd be nothing worth looting aboard.

My Fanad memories are almost all happy ones, but they do include one darker moment, an evening when my grandfather set about beating his wife with the same walking stick that had cleared our path through the ferns. Only the three of us were at the cottage at the time. I was shocked, but did speak up, with the simple words, "Alec, you shouldn't beat Betty." His eyes swivelled round to focus on me: he'd probably in his rage forgotten I was there, and he seemed to return to different reality. The beating stopped. Many years later Betty recalled this occasion, thanking me for my intervention: Alec never beat her again. Betty was heroic in her adjustment to life's misfortunes: here was a Catholic who taught my grandfather another meaning of one of Protestant Ulster's favourite words - loyalty.

Howth Perspectives

Our family's move to Howth in 1950 created a new social network. My parents' established friendships were maintained, but on a more episodic and individual basis as distance dictated; and one line of friendship in particular was to provide us with a bridge to the new suburban environment. Or so it seemed to me at the time, so my mother encouraged us all to think. George Hetherington, one of the gang who had made up parties in town, already had his home in Howth, with his wife Frances and children Frank and Lucy. The Hetherington family did come to Whitewater a couple of times, but at children's level there was caution on both sides: the Hetheringtons were no keener to get to know us than we O'Briens were to get to know them. Lucy in particular didn't conceal her distaste for the whole idea, if perhaps with a little of pouting sex appeal. Lucy bore a close resemblance to her mother: she was later to be described, by a teacher, as the <u>femme fatale</u> of Newtown School, Waterford. Frank had a face of character and although constantly nervous, he was a reflective person, someone whose judgment was worth close attention. Frank was already in his first year at Newtown School, where Lucy and I were to go the next year. This perhaps gave me good reason to turn to him for guidance. I don't know that he liked me very much, but Frank took his responsibilities seriously, and he could see that his guidance might be needed in my case. That was providential, as I was soon to owe nothing less than my continued existence to Frank's stubborn rectitude.

I couldn't have known that there would be such a payoff for me in getting to know the Hetheringtons. That rapprochement had been my mother's idea, and the Hetherington that she wanted to know was George, a dashing figure with Clark Gable good looks, dark hair and moustache and a convertible M.G. sports car. George was a poet as well as a businessman, a yachtsman and a sharpshooter. He had been to school in England, spoke with what sounded to me like a British accent. He went out of his way to engage with the O'Brien children, lots of jokes and a general good cheer. There was much that I did like in George, fun and generosity as well as entertainment, but it's also true that his presence around our family did make me a little uneasy. Conor didn't really fit into the new social picture: he was always civil to George, while George was uneasily deferential to him. I remember a moment, on the path in front of our house, when Christine pinned a fresh-cut rose to my father's lapel as he set off to work, a moment of tenderness, and a kind that was soon to disappear.

One thing my parents did seem to agree about through this period of the late 1940s and early 1950s was a negative assessment of the British. These years include the time when my father was working under Sean McBride, Minister for External Affairs, on the creation of the Irish News Agency, a time of which Conor has written somewhat ruefully and a time I remember as one of his republicanism. The British, I then gathered, were a slippery lot, not to be trusted. My mother too, an Ulster refugee in Dublin, had her own reasons to reject any idea of loyalty to Britain or the British. My parents' friends came to similar conclusions, differently reached. Christine's friend Brid Lynch, a dark-haired beauty and actress in the Abbey Theatre, talked resentfully of the Royal Academy of Dramatic Art, the stage hegemony of the upper-class English accent. George Hetherington, despite or perhaps because of his accent also had little good to say of the British.

George's wife was small, neat, and fair-haired, with a nervous kindness and gentility. She had good reason to be less than enthusiastic about us. Not only was her husband spending as much time with Christine as he could get away with, he was spending more time with the O'Brien children than his own. Frank and Lucy would have taken their mother's part, and George's posture in their company could be painful to see: bonhomie is an ugly Gallicism that might just about cover it, his blustering geniality papered over a fault line. Lucy in return was openly scornful, while Frank's nervous talk skirted around his own reservations: put it another way, Frank kept his views about his father to himself. I remember one or two visits to the Hetherington home, the well-polished wood, the carpets and the neatness, a long-playing record of the musical <u>Salad Days</u>. Frank had a great set of toy trains, but wasn't that interested in them. He told me of his father's shooting the stalks of the tulips in their garden: noting his mother's displeasure, but he did share George's enthusiasm for yachting.

The emptiness of the Hetherington home, the loss of warmth at the centre, had its counterpart higher up Howth Hill, in Whitewater. I slept in the front sun-porch of that house, with a splendid view over Dublin Bay; behind me were French windows, on the other side of which was my parents' bedroom. Conor and Christine kept up their social talk in the rest of the house, maybe a little edgy but with a joke or two, some irony, and banter about politics, current affairs or culture. However, when the bedroom door was closed, and all talk gave way to silence, I overheard not a word, so I knew as much as I wanted to know (which wasn't much) about my parents' marriage. Perhaps they kept silent because they knew I was there, but the social chill did seep out to me under those glass doors. I loved my front sun porch/bedroom, the nautical chart of Dublin Bay on the wall, the bay and the hills of Counties Dublin and Wicklow before me, the foghorn and the buoys as well as the howl of the wind, the lighthouses and the ships. So I didn't worry that much about the silence behind me. The prospect of going to boarding school could have been dark enough, in that transition year, 1950-51, but I don't remember any dread: certainly nothing like the outburst of tears on the imminence of primary school. Problems at home and that chill through the French doors may have been helpful here. There was no Garden of Eden, no more, at Howth Summit, so why not give boarding school a try?

CHAPTER 3

Apprenticeship in Migration: Boarding School

A Quaker Education

Why was I sent, for my secondary education, to Newtown School Waterford? My parents' explanation was the same as the choice for my primary education: Quaker schooling - tolerant of the agnostic. I wouldn't have to go to classes in religion, nor to Sunday service. Good news so far, but why in boarding school, a hundred miles from Dublin? Frank Hetherington was already in Newtown: that would make things easier for me, Lucy would be going too. That explanation or justification looked good enough at the time, but I wasn't too happy about the idea of going to boarding school: it just looked like something that had to be done.

Looking back on that moment now, knowing a little more of the family forces that were at work around me, it may be possible to make a little more sense of what still looks like a confusing situation. The first point is that my mother, even with the Hetherington involvement, was not at all pleased at the idea of my going to boarding school. When my sister Fedelma's turn came, four years later, she refused point-blank to go to that school, threatening to lie down on the platform at

Kingsbridge Station and howl: I never thought of that. The second point in my own case is that the driving force affecting my parents' decision was apparently the advice of Owen Sheehy Skeffington, elder cousin and surrogate father to Conor. Owen stressed Newtown's tolerance and good morals, as well as education, but I now wonder if he didn't have some other things also in mind. He was a shrewd person, there's nobody with whom Conor would have shared more confidence. Together they could perhaps see the point of getting this ten year old away from too close scrutiny of a marriage in severe difficulty.

My mini-migration, to the suburb of a town on the south coast of Ireland, looked substantial to this small Dubliner. Once I was there I was in an enclosed social world, well out of range of casual visits from family or friends. My family came dutifully at half-terms, took me out to the sea at Tramore or Dunmore East, and otherwise came rarely enough. The first journey to school began at Kingsbridge Station. Frank Hetherington and I took refuge in boyish ideas of stoicism as there were other children's tears on the station platform. My own lamentation was the night before, at home. When we arrived in Waterford, the town didn't look very appealing: a quay-side by the river Suir, the very old Reginald's tower and not a lot else. I needn't have been concerned, for in school we weren't going to be allowed to see much of Waterford anyway.

The school grounds defined the limits of my life for the next six years. The new arrivals, and the rest of the school, were welcomed by the Headmaster, William Glynn, a man of immediate moral authority, defining our world as it ought to be. In the school meeting every morning we would get a short reading from the Bible, sing a hymn or two, and then hear what the Head had to tell us for the day. And I did get the message that religion meant order. But this didn't convert me into an instant believer, a better person, or even a perfect hypocrite, but it did suggest a second thought about my parents' agnostic belief. Initially the reality of boarding school, away from the reassuring discipline of the morning meeting, seemed to me very confusing. I remember a moment, not long after arriving when I stood in the corner of the school yard and called out the name of the only boy I knew: "Hetherington!" Frank did come from somewhere, looking a bit embarrassed on my behalf, and gave me the voice of a year's Newtown experience: "Donal, just do what the other boys do." That advice I was to find impossible to follow: even at the time of hearing his well-meant words, I doubted that they would be much help to me.

A further memory, a couple of years on, suggests part of the problem: it is of being pulled by the hair down the school corridor. Bertie Allen was shorter than me, but bulkier and better co-ordinated: his words as he pulled me: "O'Brien, ye're so <u>stubborn</u>." Bertie was no sadist, just a bit impatient with the wrong-headed. The school was no lawless jungle. But it also wasn't the well-ordered collectivity suggested by the morning assembly.

One Newtown old boy, whom I was to meet long afterwards at a dinner party in London, reacted with vehemence to my mention of the school. That place, he said as he slammed his hand down on the dining table, was like Dachau. He didn't want another word said on the subject. Perry Anderson had lived with his family in Waterford. He and his brother Benedict would have attended Newtown before my time. They both became journalists and scholars - pillars of the New Left in London. To see Newtown as a concentration camp seemed a bit odd to me: maybe Perry hadn't much taste for games, or it was just that he was too good at his books, and maybe not good enough at hiding his book learning. Those are the zones of inquiry that came to mind, but a dinner party of New Left chic was not the place to ask.

That brings me back to the twin subjects of religion and the school's headmaster. William Glynn presided over the assembly: grey/white hair, an erect bearing, serious - the incarnation of Quaker values. I remember his tread as he came across the gravel from his house to the assembly, like God with flat feet. He did not talk much about purely religious subjects during the morning assembly. As a pacifist and conscientious objector to the First World War he had been a stretcher-bearer and medical assistant to the troops: we were sure that he had been very brave, and were convinced that the medical teams had been exposed to just as much danger as the fighting soldiers. Perhaps they had: he never said so, but we needed to believe that it was so.

Glynn taught some French as well as religion, but his principal function was as figure of authority. He was a sort of part-time father to me: not that I didn't have a perfectly good father back home, but Conor was a hundred miles away. Glynn advised me in my second-last year, for example, to wait a while before reading Balzac, wait and be a little older: good advice, delivered without condescension (or any sense of disapproval of Balzac). He set the moral compass: on the importance of telling the truth (you can get confused, and contradict yourself, when you start telling lies); on the importance of looking after yourself (you can't help others much if you don't help yourself first). There was a Quaker validation of silence every morning, giving one time to think. I do remember, towards the end of my time at Newtown, questioning the pacifist stance for those confronted by Adolf Hitler. Glynn reacted by looking down, didn't say a word.

I was to come away from Newtown with a great respect for Quaker values: some Quakers could be smug, but on the whole, they were as a group modest and charitable people. They were also capable of decisive action. There was an occasion when one of the boys, whose parents were Christian scientists, became acutely ill and needed an operation to save his life. The parents told the headmaster that they didn't want medical interference. Glynn replied that the boy was in school, of which he was headmaster, and that the operation should proceed. There was an operation, and the boy survived; I am sure to the parents' great relief.

During my first school holidays, I secured my parents' permission to take the class in religion in the new term. Glynn taught that class with the sayings and doings of Jesus Christ including a generous commentary on the Sermon on the

Mount. The attraction of Quaker faith and of a religious outlook more generally was the structure of social order with which it was accompanied. We pupils weren't in a war of all against all, not quite; there were the prefects to relay the authority of the teachers, but the idea of an orderly world had its appeal. I learned something fundamental in Newtown something that was to be with me for the rest of my life, a sympathetic approach to religious belief (even if, for me, God didn't quite come into it).

I was promoted a form after questioning the school text's proposition that the Mississippi-Missouri was the longest river in the world. "Not so," said I, "that's counting two rivers as one". I certainly wasn't the first pupil to realize that, but it was enough for a promotion. So began my reputation in Newtown as a swot. Sammy McClure, the geography teacher, may have been favourably impressed, but among the other pupils it never paid to stand out in class. You paid after the class was over: a lesson which took a lot of time for me to learn fully. "Swot," "teacher's pet", all of that and more meant that I was losing ground among my peers. I remember an occasion when I got involved in an exchange of (ineffectual) blows with a fellow-pupil: there was a lot of cheering from the other pupils, but most of the applause was for my opponent. To realize that you aren't very popular is painful, even if you might have known it already.

There are ways, though, that even a swot can fight back in the arena of classroom opinion. One way of course was to keep your hand down, but that was difficult in classes I liked, with teachers I respected. Another way would have been to do well in games, rugby most of all, but that was beyond me at this time. Then there was classroom insubordination, to work on vulnerable and/or unpopular teachers: I got quite good at this kind of unpleasantness. You could also make a point of doing as little as possible, reading your adventure stories under the desk during maths class. That kind of studied indolence may have helped to overcome the swot image with my classmates, but in the longer run it was of course self-defeating. Mr. Foster, our teacher of Irish, pulled me up short. One afternoon in the school corridor, we passed one another and he turned and said, "You could make something of yourself, O'Brien, if you'd only do a day's work."

That was a timely observation. I was 13 years old, a year away from taking my first state exams, for the Intermediate Certificate. F.E.F., to use the initials by which Mr. Foster was known throughout the school, didn't go into any of that: no lecture, no threat, just a wistful observation. F.E.F. was a generous person, a teacher who took a real interest in his pupils, well beyond what his duty required. He and his wife hosted evenings for senior pupils, one might call them soirees, a hint of gracious living and some very good conversation. He also worked very hard to keep the school running, and I think he wanted me to learn something central to his own life: that work makes you feel better about yourself. He never said that, just demonstrated by example. It was flattering at thirteen to have the attention of an important teacher, and to hear that he awarded me a possibly successful future. It was even reassuring in a way that he thought there was something amusing in my situation. He conveyed that life was a challenge, the kind of thing I'd been reading about in all those adventure books. So it seemed obvious: one met the challenge. Not that my own reaction to F.E.F.'s words was as prompt as it might have been in an adventure story. I still had my classroom reputation to consider, my vulnerability of going red in the face for example. It was those looming state exams which were beginning to shift the weight of classroom preoccupation. It's not each of us against the others, it's each of us against an impersonal examiner, for the sake our own future. The swot was beginning to emerge.

History was by some distance my favourite class. Eileen Webster, the teacher, had the gift of keeping the class's interest by the quality of what she had to say. She never a raised her voice and there was never impertinence on ours. Mrs. Webster was middle-aged, maternal in appearance, radiating a gentle intelligence and kind humour. Our textbook for the history of Ireland included a fair amount of nationalist sentiment. She didn't contradict the text, or even gently mock the sentiment, but rather pointed to ways in which we might illustrate the key points by considering the matter from the point of view of the people involved. Geography was another class I enjoyed: Sammy McClure, another teacher with good classroom presence, really wanted us to get the map of England right. His brother had a farm across the border in Northern Ireland; Sammy had a small-holding of its own, and we believed that they did good business in smuggling animals across the border, which only added to Sammy's authority. Mathematics does not bear a mention: red-faced Mr. Boggs didn't have much patience with slow learners like me. In Irish too I struggled, for all of F.E.F.'s charm and cajoling: "pure parrot learning, O'Brien."

Newtown Incidents and Adventures

Before studying, however, you also have to stay alive, and I came close to failing there. I had been suffering for some weeks from stomach pains. They were getting worse, but the school nurse wasn't interested. She was apparently more interested in our games master than in the complaints of tiresome little boys. It got to a point where Frank Hetherington spotted me going across the school yard bent double. He went straight to an older ex-nurse who still lived at the School, Ma Robinson and asked her to come and see me. Ma Robinson immediately called the school doctor; who ran his finger across the side of my lower abdomen and called an ambulance. My appendix apparently burst in the ambulance, and the doctor performed a life-saving operation when I arrived at the local hospital. The nuns took very good care of me, and apparently they said prayers for me back at school. But the successful outcome had most to do with Frank's good sense, appraisal and action. It did feel good to be alive in that hospital/nursing home, with a view of the river Suir, with the occasional ship going by from Waterford to the sea. Coming exams didn't cross my mind: a close encounter with your own death is another kind of scrutiny.

When I did get back to school it was to an altered social environment, a change for the better. It wasn't exactly that people were surprised to see me back, but it seemed I had earned more respect owing to my ordeal. This may have been the time from when I began to enjoy school. There was the little matter of realizing how good it was to be alive, but there was other encouragement. I began to get a little better at sport - swimming and rugby in particular. I was picked to play as full back in the game against our local Protestant rival, Bishop Foy's School. We were leading by 12 points to 9 towards the end of the match when the biggest of their backs, Micky Davis, broke through and headed for the line. He wasn't a good runner, but he was quite a bit more muscular than me: I brought him down; we won the match and on leaving the pitch I was treated to the admiration of some of the onlookers. That tackle meant more to me than success in any exam at the time. The term report from the games master, which noted that I had made the full back position my own, made its impression on both my parents.

There was a notable incident about this time which may give some flavour of life in boarding school. I was passing the school kitchen when I saw two older boys having a mock fight. One of the boys, Ian Gibson, in an impulsive gesture aimed the contents of a cup of coffee at the other and missed: the liquid went all over the wall. I moved on. The next morning in assembly, the headmaster announced that somebody had thrown coffee over the school kitchen wall. Unless that somebody came forward, the day's school walk would be cancelled. Nobody did come forward, and I certainly wasn't going to "help the police with their inquiries": there was a clear schoolboy ethic on such things. And there was also the fact that Gibson and Alan Pym were both a lot bigger than me. Ian was a stylish person, tall, with a good physique, and plenty of brown curly hair. He walked and talked with assurance. He was good at games as well as at his books: he even read us some saucy passages from Chaucer at night in the dorm. I told no one about what I had seen, but did share in the school's resentment of the loss of that day's outing: those unsupervised walks were a treat for us all, as well as being an occasion for some of the boys and girls to get to know each other a little better. So we all resented whoever it was, and I resented Ian Gibson. He went on to do very well in life: living in Spain, he was an expert in Spanish literature, the biographer of the poet Lorca and something of a star of the Madrid cultural scene. In conversation with my wife Rita I would give Ian the tag line, "the man who threw the coffee on the school kitchen wall," but never explained the circumstances. So, at a reception in Madrid, we met Ian for a moment apart from his important friends, and Rita delivered the tag line, "Ian Gibson, a man who..." I had read the phrase, "He went white" in books before, but had never witnessed it personally. When Ian had recovered himself a little, he muttered, "It was cocoa.... how did you know?" If we were a film, that would be the moment to roll the credits.

In the process of getting older and bigger, I became less easy to push around (or pull by the hair). There was a summer camp at Caragh Lake in Kerry, to which some boys would be invited each year, no girls. We were housed in a corrugated metal boathouse next to a cottage owned by Wilson Strangman, a friend of Newtown School, an author. Eight of us slept on mattresses on the floor, spent our days in agreeable idleness, jumping into the lake from the pier next to the boathouse, rowing about in a lazy manner, trailing a fishing line and even sometimes catching a trout or an eel. The more energetic climbed mountains: we weren't far from Carrantuohill, the highest mountain in Ireland, but there were very few takers for such expeditions. In the evenings we would eat the catch of the day, and soda bread, bought at a shop a mile or so up the river.

Mr. Strangman's expectation, in return for the invitation to this pleasant retreat, was that on one occasion during our fortnight stay we boys would accompany him for a photography session. We rowed him up a stream with good overhang from rhododendron bushes; he set up his tripod, with black cloth pulled over his head, a big camera ready. What we boys then had to do was to take off all our clothes, sit about on the rocks, and click, click. What we were given to understand was that Mr. Strangman was interested in experimental photography, effects of light and shade. At the time I don't think any of us questioned that. We didn't talk about it among ourselves, although later there was certainly a raised eyebrow or two. Wilson Strangman, his tripod, the cloth, his white hair and his decrepit stance (something like Great Uncle Bulgaria from "The Wombles") was perhaps good for an indulgent smile. They School knew him to be harmless, no doubt, but was he dabbling in pornography during these holidays?

I was invited to Caragh Lake by Strangman over a supper of sausages and chips at the Savoy Cinema in Waterford, the first time I ever tasted tomato ketchup. Such an invitation was an important marker of Newtown status, more important than editing the school magazine or acting in the school play. Running the school tuck shop together with Joyce Jackson that was much more fun: I was becoming part of the social action. The arrival of rock 'n roll in our school dances livened things up a bit with the girls. No wild anarchy to be sure, but an emergence from the typical gender apartheid of our co-educational school. We kept up to date through Radio Luxembourg and the American Forces Network from which I learned one of my all-time favourite songs:

> *Now a pterodactyl child was a flying fool,*
> *Just a breeze flapping daddy of the old-school,*
> *But if and when a mamadactyl made him drool, he went*
> *"Aah-eeh-aah", ape call,*
> *Don't be a cube, Rube, go ape.*
>
> *Now Adam was the first man in the land,*
> *A be-zorch daddy with an iron hand,*
> *But when little Eve said "hiya man",*
> *He went...*

Not many people seemed to know about the singer, Nervous Norvus either in Newtown or the wider world of Dublin. I was a bit ahead of the game, and could sing it from memory with a bloodcurdling Ape Call.

I was still a bit scared of girls, for all of that bravado, and when invited on a raid on the girls' dorm turned that chance

7. At home from boarding school

down. It was the night before I was to make a long planned bicycle ride back 113 miles to Howth. The journey took me seven and a half hours, not bad given that all I'd brought was a bottle of Lucozade. The night-time raiders, including most of the top people, were caught: and thus disqualified themselves from becoming prefects the following year. I had not been a top person, but thus it was that I became prefect in my last year at school, with the silver badge of pre-eminence (top person by default). I was a bit startled to hear sometime after leaving school that some people had looked on me as a bully in my role.

Leaving school just before my 17th birthday in 1958 was a relief, leaving behind a social world in which status had depended so heavily on how good you were at games. The words of our gym teacher, Mr. Fraser, on seeing me try to vault the gymnasium horse, haunt me still: "The *idea* is there, but the execution is *crrrude*." The humiliation of that horse would be no more.

Thinking about England

Books could count for more now, as there was no more need to hide the fact that you were interested in them. I was comfortable with books; they had been my escape from the reality of life in boarding school and took me away, far away. Captain W.E. Johns' many adventures of Biggles flying for the Royal Air Force in the Second World War; those had been my solace after I grew out of the comics. It was a very British kind of escape. There was Arthur Conan Doyle - Professor Challenger as well as Sherlock Homes, John Buchan too. We read Dickens as part of school assignment). Macbeth was required for the Intermediate Certificate, Hamlet for Leaving. And at one time I did know some lines of Milton's Paradise Lost by heart, including "Better to reign in Hell than serve in Heaven" - not a bad line for the school prefect.

While I had read my share of English stories and taken in my share of anti-British sentiment, I knew very little of life across the water. Benny Marshall didn't talk about his experience of living in Birmingham working as a milk maid, nor did Dermot Mullane tell how he came by his English accent. My best friend in the last two years at Newtown was Dave McEwan who came originally from Scotland. Dave and I did a lot of talking; we listened to "Hancock's Half Hour". Tony Hancock could double me up with his depressed humour.

What did I know of England, or Britain, apart from my school lessons and readings, with snippets of information from family conversation and a few fellow pupils? As one looks over the range of other sources, the answer has to be, quite a lot: certainly more than most immigrants to the United Kingdom in more recent times. First of all there was the English language, the only idiom. Then there was the radio, English humour coming to devoted school audiences for "The Goon Show" (1954-58): Major Bloodnok, General Cash My Cheque, Harry Seagoon, and the inspired Peter Sellers. This kind of humour - poking fun at established ways - can be seen as an invitation into British culture: self-mockery, being an English means of seduction. We were already half engaged in a process of what could be called Anglicisation, assimilation, or "selling out" on what we were taught in some of our school books was our Irish national culture.

Newtown pupils spent a lot of our spare time listening to the BBC which brought us "Journey into Space", as well as the news of the Suez crisis in 1956. Most of my class were for Nasser as he was against the Brits. Some of us bought The Observer on Sunday, the principal newspaper which campaigned against the Anglo-French invasion (and lost a third of its circulation in consequence). We also enjoyed Alec Guiness and the Ealing comedies, "The Ladykillers" for example, the English laughing at themselves. The English books that we read for pleasure were P.G. Wodehouse and Ian Fleming.

"British" for practical purposes meant "English" so far as I was concerned at this time. "Welsh" was off the map, and "Scottish" too tangled up with my mother's family background. The British were "them", which meant that "they" were essentially English. Quite a few Irish people mean "the English" when they say "the Brits." About the English I got mixed messages. At school, there was a television in the assembly hall which was acquired so we could watch the Queen's coronation in 1953. It was the first time any of us had seen TV. No one seemed to mind the screening of an English coronation. I was enough of a budding Irish nationalist to wonder what was going on, but enough also of a new boy to keep my mouth tight shut. Some of the Newtown teachers had lived or been trained in England. Mrs. Webster was at her very best teaching about the 17th century English Civil War. Oliver

Cromwell was seen in Ireland, as among the worst of our oppressors, understandably so: but we needed also to understand what he represented in terms of the internal divisions of English society, of the international politics of the time, and the coming of parliamentary supremacy.

So Brits not all bad, and certainly not all the same kind of bad (or good) at school: Newtown even had a sister school in England, Layton Park. Britain, England, these were facts of life, and we were never taught to look in their direction with real enmity. We could of course bring our own resentments, of Britain's wealth and power, of the historical misdeeds recalled in our textbooks and of English upper-class arrogance. You could call that an Irish inferiority complex, given voice in the patriotic ballads that I sang with enthusiasm at this time. The Clancy Brothers "Roddie McCorley Goes to Die on the Bridge of Toome today"; "Another Martyr for Old Ireland, Another Murder for the Crown;" "Kevin Barry gave his young life for the cause of liberty"...ah, the delicious self-pity of all that. In Howth village the Abbey Tavern made a speciality of Republican ballads, attracting camaraderie of the armchair supporters of the IRA. I did go to the Abbey a few times on some of my last holidays from school and I bought a record of the Clancy Brothers and Tommy Makem: so at the age of 15 I might have been considered a bit of an armchair Republican myself.

This fatal attraction did not entirely disappear, even with a lot more years and what should be described as better sense. The night after writing the last line in the previous paragraph (31

March 2009), I had a dream that brought back Newtown School and my Irish enthusiasm of 50 years ago. In that dream Roy Foster, a good friend of my adult years in London, F.E.F.'s son and also a Newtown old boy, as well is being the biographer of W.B.Yeats and a leading historian of Ireland tells me that "He can't see what's the problem." I tell him that "You know damn well what's the problem. The Brits are the problem. We should drive out the Brits." At this point Roy's wife Aisling (a novelist and critic) touches my arm to make a practical point, "Donal, we don't have the numbers." And then I wake up in bed in our home in Dorset, having lived very comfortably in England all my adult life.

That's a dream which takes a bit of explanation. I first saw Roy Foster as a little boy with a Cheshire cat smile in Newtown's corridor; as he was being shown around by his father prior to enrolling in school. His hand was in his fathers: two smiles in a dusty corridor. I was about to leave Newtown, as Roy was about to start. Roll the clock on, 30 years, and we have Professor Foster, living in London, teaching in Oxford. By now this historian of Ireland is widely identified as a "revisionist" in his approach to our nationalist pieties, no friend to militant republicanism. Aisling too has a subversive sense of humour, subverting (among other things) those same pieties. In my waking hours, and most agreeably when in their company, that's where I stand too: some of the best of laughter has been in their company, looking back to school days, to childhood, to life. So the dream could be seen as a darker extension of that conversation; but then what kind of a revisionist is the writer of these lines?

The blood-thirsty subconscious of Quaker-educated Donal perhaps requires explanation also at another level, the relationship between father and son. Conor had I think an unanswerable claim as being the father also of what has come to be called revisionism in the writing of Irish history. When not lost in my mysterious sub-conscious I fully supported his line, especially on the Protestants of Northern Ireland, my mother's people. It just won't do to try to bomb and blackmail them into a United Ireland. Sigmund Freud would no doubt give a nod here, this is only what's to be expected: maybe so, wise old man, now let me try to redeem myself by telling it as straight as I can.

No sooner had I set down this resolve then I enjoyed another dream (8 April 2009). This time I was at the entrance to different camps, enclosed by wooden fencing as in a film of the old West, the identity of each camp indicated by a wooden sign over the entry, black letters that looked as though they had been burned into the wood. In front of me is "British Camp;" I turn aside, next to it is "Irish Camp." I look in: it's crowded, a lot of people are shouting and waving, I pull back. There's another camp, but I can't read the sign, so find myself walking tentatively into the British camp, wondering what am I doing here? The British Camp doesn't have a lot of people near the entrance; there is no guard, but some soldiers in the distance. In the foreground children's toys are scattered on the grass, and a small plastic slide that I recognize as looking like the one we've installed in the garden for the grandchildren. Then I wake up.

What I think the first dream reveals is something abject in myself, going back if not to infancy then at least to school days. I remember the way in which I would support any national team against England. My mother thought that was going a bit far: supporting the Springbocks? At school, it was depressing to me to have to listen to England doing well in cricket against the West Indies, including P.B.H. May and Colin Cowdray batting forever. Resentment of England, with its significant portion of envy, is not something to which I'd wakefully admit.

Continental Horizons

In 1955 my father became Councillor in the Irish Embassy in Paris, and the family moved (for a little over a year) to a small suburban house on the river at La Frette sur Seine. The treat was to watch the barge traffic going up and down. My sisters did not like the local French school and told me I was better off at boarding school. My mother missed George Hetherington and my father went in for some heavy drinking: a miserable time for all the family of which I saw little. In school we'd been doing the French Revolution and Napoleon, I'd been reading a little of Stendhal and was for a time captivated by the epic of revolutionary France, as told by French novelists and historians. The bad guys were undoubtedly the English: Pitt the younger and the paid agents of aristocracy in their unceasing conspiracy to suppress the cause of the revolution: money versus freedom.

In sport I turned my enthusiasm to the support of French cycling, applauding Jacques Anquetil in his many times winning of the Tour de France, and began to learn some serious French. I fixed up an elaborate aerial on the roof of Whitewater in order to follow it on French radio stations, and I subscribed to Le Miroir des Sports. My French wasn't bad, but with a rather specialized vocabulary: peloton, echappée, crevaison, I'd be okay there, but you shouldn't ask me in French about ballroom dancing, gardening, or the inner life of loneliness.

I was also, in this period, beginning to do some international cycling of my own, touring first in the Rhine valley (1956), then the Loire Valley (1957). These tours were in the summer holidays, a group of four riders, including Helmut Clissmann, Frank Hetherington. Helmut was effectively team leader in 1956, he spoke German, but the rest of the team didn't take to Germany much: too much cycling near to the heavy lorries that were accelerating the country's economic recovery. I subsequently learned that the management of the youth hostels we used were in the post-war period often run by ex-Nazis. It did feel like that. The next year in France I was team leader on the same grounds of relative language competence. The hostels were less orderly than in Germany; there were less lorries and it was a lot more agreeable to all except Helmut. There was a moment, meandering across Normandy, when Frank wanted us to make a detour to see the site of the D-Day landings. Helmut was very much opposed to this: I think he did mutter something about Brits. My call and I came down for Helmut. Maybe it was laziness, not wanting to do the extra kilometres, maybe it was loyalty to my old friend, but maybe too I didn't then think the D-Day landings were any of my national business: for my shame.

My family looked outward in their reading, and encouraged me to look far and wide. In France, we visited a lot of cathedrals accessible on day trips from Paris. In 1955 we went on a joint family holiday to Northern Spain with the Hetherington's: a tense occasion. The two sets of parents gave up on that idea thereafter: there was no repetition of fake togetherness. England or Britain were in any case not tourist destinations in this period. Conor's new posting, from 1956 to 1960 was to the Irish delegation at the United Nations in New York, although he was home-based for most of the year. I remember that Conor found excitement in his United Nations job: he was much happier than he had been in Paris. Christine too was happier to be back in Dublin, as were Fedelma and Kate.

Back Home in Ireland

In those last years of school when home on holiday (1956-58) I did a lot of bird-watching around the Howth cliffs. When you got too near to gulls' nests you would be dive-bombed by them. I would take the hint, move away. I took personal pride in the pair of Northern Guillemots nesting on the cliffs near the Baily lighthouse, and loved to watch the birds that would skim the sea surface below: fulmars, shearwaters, guillemots.

There was an occasion, climbing up the cliff from Whitewater Cove with two friends when one of them froze 6 feet from the top, 200 feet above the rocks below. We did cajole our companion up those last few feet. The boy may have been right to hesitate, it was a tricky passage, but it would have been worse for him to try to climb back down. I definitely wouldn't want my grandson going anywhere near those cliffs. We climbed by hanging onto the grass for the most part: it was lucky for us that the grass was tough stuff, well rooted. We did a lot of swimming, usually at Whitewater cove, where I would show off my diving.

I sailed with George Hetherington in his Dragon. I don't know why George was devoted to yacht racing, why one uncomfortable racing class yacht was to succeed another. It seemed to me that he always lost the race, usually by a substantial margin. For his crew it was a pleasure to get out on the sea, to watch the sea birds, the clouds, the land viewed from changing angles, to feel the wind. But when racing with George, serving as crew under his captaincy, these gentle pleasures were always mitigated by tension. George was good at the peremptory command, "Ready about", "Lee, ho", shifting his weight from one side to the other, with his captain's cap on. Back on shore, Fedelma did mutter something about Captain Bligh. There was one occasion to recall against the charge of tyranny, when I was crew together with a school friend on a day of gale force winds. The race was an important one, and for once George got us into a very clear lead, while both of the crew were getting violently sick overboard. As we neared Howth harbour and got ready for the second round of the course, George looked compassionately at the crew and turned into port. The crew didn't object: I knew how much he would have loved to win that race. To me that was Captain George's finest hour.

On school holidays there were also the visits to see my grandfather, first in Belfast, then in Ballinaclash, County Wicklow. Alec and Betty were to have three children, John, Mary, and Brian: so I now had two uncles and an aunt, all younger than myself. The house in Clash came with a farm, 60 acres of Wicklow hillside. A local man, Tom Cullen, took care of such farming as there was: a very large white sow, revelling in the muck of the yard, was Alec's main interest. Alec taught Betty Latin. He talked to me about the Iliad, about the ancient Greeks in general, conveying easily his fascination. But he never tried to be my teacher, and I think that was just as well. I loved my grandfather, but he had a peremptory manner which might have put me off the classics forever. Alec, now a Catholic, took that commitment seriously, but he remained scornful of the priests' Latin. Our family made regular Sunday visits, driving down across some beautiful hillsides. I stayed in Clash once for a week and Tom Cullen taught me to plough with horses: he was a patient teacher, but I think he could see that this pupil wasn't going far. So we kicked a football around instead.

Looking back on this period in my life, the boarding school years of 1951-58, it may be time to review the evidence for the notion that school was perhaps an apprenticeship for migration. One should beware, I know, of inserting retrospective logic into previous experience. I certainly had very little idea where I was going, or what I was going to do.

To go to boarding school does involve separation from one's family, from one's mother I think most importantly. But for comfort I had Christine's almost daily letters, the biscuits, fruit, and chocolate that came in parcels to replenish the "tuck box" that each pupil hoarded. There were the half-term holiday visits from my family. I remember the glamorous broad brimmed hat my mother wore on one of her visits, a touch of Lauren Bacall amidst the Quaker mothers' millinery: little conventionalist that I was, I wished that she had dressed more like them.

I greatly looked forward to the half-term visits above all for the better food that was in store. A trip to the seaside would be part of that, and meals at the local beach-side hotels. The Grand Hotel, Tramore, was my favourite, raffish, seedy, perhaps to some people, down at heal. The Grand stood at the end of a long beach, vertically facing a half-mile row of sand dunes: these were the dunes where one might hope for a moment's concealment with one of the girls on our unsupervised school walks and with luck a little fumbling about. The food would be properly cooked: I enjoyed the fish and chips. And not all of it boiled, as was school's kitchen's preference: boil a cabbage for a very long time, then leave it standing in the water, slop it out to the little brats when the time comes. They won't complain. I write with bitterness here, the living memory of indignant "victimhood".

The experience of boarding school amounted to a preparation for migration, to my mind. My two sisters went to day schools in Dublin, and it was in Dublin that they stayed, married, and set up home. I felt a stranger in Dublin after an interval of six years in boarding school. But there still was nothing inevitable about my migration, nor was the boarding school background necessarily a propellant to England. The Donal who left Newtown School had some creditable results in those state examinations behind him, he had been well taught, and he was looking for the main chance.

CHAPTER 4

Swotting Around: A Student in Paris and Dublin

On my Bike in Paris

You could still cycle around the <u>Arc de Triomphe</u> in Paris in 1958, in the middle of the day. Although there were few fellow-cyclists, the car hadn't yet totally taken over. As I wobbled up the <u>Avenue des Champs Elysée</u>, and even, at some peril, around the <u>Étoile</u>, I could soak up the imperial grandeur, while keeping an eye out for gaps in the traffic. The Avenue and the Arc were to an extent familiar to me as the Irish Embassy wasn't far from the <u>Étoile</u>. My father had pointed out that the very long list of Napoleon's victorious battles, carved into the stone, was misleading: many of the victories had been draws at best, some were outright defeats for the French, and the victories were very often against the Austrians, a disunited army. So I knew that all might not be quite as it was presented on the grand façades. But it's one thing to be escorted around the sights by your very well-informed father, to be driven about in the comfortable family car, another to be cycling around on your own in the face of all that show of power. Napoleon, now there was a migrant who had made his mark: I wasn't thinking quite in those terms at the time, but the Corsican's imperial career did have its power to fascinate a young man. You didn't even have to be French. It was also one thing to have been in Paris (mostly the suburbs) with my family, as in 1955-56, another to be there as a student, a lot more centrally located and on my own. I was now enrolled as a student in what was then the <u>École des Sciences Politiques.</u> <u>Sciences Po'</u>, as it was familiarly known, was just off the Boulevard St. Germain, near to the heart of the city's Left Bank. So there I was, fresh out of Newtown School Waterford, 17 years of age, placed in a postgraduate class for foreigners, most of them at least five years older than myself.

It was of course Conor who had made this unusual situation possible. He had known the Director of <u>Sciences Po'</u>, had asked what could be done for me in what would now be called a gap year, to give me a chance to learn some French and maybe even some political science. The Director had chosen the postgraduate class as the best option ("they're not so fussy about credentials") so down I came, on the Director's parachute, into this group of what looked to me like quite mature students. My fellow-students (the most approachable of them American) treated me for the most part with an amused tolerance, but an age gap of five years made anything like friendship difficult to imagine on either side of the gulf in years. My studies didn't add up to anything very much. I did attend some lectures, as well as a weekly seminar/tutorial, but didn't get that much out of the lectures, even of what I could understand. There was one occasion when our teacher held up one of the class essays, dangling it by thumb and forefinger (recognizably my scrawly script) and asked, "Who wrote this?" The script in question was a denunciation of the French

Socialist Party leader Guy Mollet. Our teacher, I later learned, was a party militant. The essay was visibly more than a bit of a mess, the blotches produced by my leaky fountain pen could be seen by the rest of the class, inviting a moment of derision for the author. And the lesson of it all was duly delivered by our teacher, that the essay's polemic had no place in our class: "en sciences politiques, on ne fait pas de jugement de valeur" (best said in French). There were some in the class, mainly Americans ready to come to my defence: one of them mentioned Socrates, persecuted for telling the truth. To me that was going a bit far, but the class broke up in some disorder. The teacher's last word to me was that I might write something worth reading, at a later time, in my own language.

I learned more at Sciences Po' by joining up for the school's rugby team. Although still not very good at playing rugby, I was young, keen, physically fit – at least enough to keep my place on the team as either wing forward or full back. We weren't a very good team, but we did play every week, we did train together, and when we spoke to each other, it was in no other language than French. And we spoke quite a lot, coming and going to grounds in the Paris suburbs. That's how I really learned to speak French, following the French that was spoken by French people among themselves, the slang, the curses, and the hurly-burly of a rugby repertoire. I still made mistakes in speaking, but the rugby team didn't pull you up short with a correction or condescension: one just kept going. So you can build up a bit of confidence, away from the school or college bench and feel some of the fun of speaking French. I owe a lot to those rugby-playing political scientists, a helping hand towards a surer use of their language: speaking French could be a buzz. One of those players, in recognition of something I had done on the pitch (clearly under pressure) called me "l'irlandais au sang froid," good to hear at my tender age.

When I say that we political scientists didn't make up a very good rugby team, that's telling the truth, but also hiding an anomaly: one of our players was really good, had been a professional in rugby league, even I think an international. His surname was Schwander, he played centre three-quarter: he was very strong, fast and creative. When he got the ball the game took a whole different shape, the opposition reeled: so the political scientists' game plan was a simple one....... get the ball to Schwander. Thanks to that gifted player we even won some of our matches: observing the rest of us at play, Schwander at times would give a rueful shake of the head. What he was doing among us still puzzles me. Was he not enjoying his studies, or did he just feel the need of a little gentle exercise? He added a dignity to our proceedings that the rest of us scarcely earned. The fact that he showed up at all for our matches was a bit like a patronising clap on the back for the rest of us, and we did feel the better for it.

I had felt lonely on first arriving in Paris in September 1958, installed in a room on the Rue Gay Lussac, close to the Jardins de Luxembourg. That was an excellent location for a student, within walking distance of the École des Sciences Politiques: the room had been found for me by a friend of my parents, Mark Mortimer, who worked in Paris for the British Council. Mark had been a fellow student of theirs at Trinity College

Dublin, a tennis partner among other things, a brave man who had lost an arm but still played a good game of tennis. He had lost a good deal of his sandy brown hair, a man with a ready smile to go with a slightly anxious look. Within two days of my arrival I got back to him with a cry for help. It had been good the first day to get up, walk to the café on the corner, order a café au lait and a croissant, and be part of the big city scene. But what then? I didn't know anybody my own age: wasn't there somewhere to live that would put me more into contact with other people of my own age? Mortimer came to my rescue, using his British Council weight to get me a room out in the Cité Universitaire in the Madison Franco-Britanie. So it was Britain that came to the rescue of this lonely young Irishman. There I found an abundance of people not more than a year or two older than myself, most of them British but also including some Irish students. In that Maison, the English language ruled. I had some English friends, even a Hungarian, Sandor, who had his own little motor car.

Life was looking up, there was coming and going in my room, including one Irish visitor who had the status of folk hero in bourgeois Dublin (even if very few knew who he was, a great many were grateful for what he had done). A ghastly piece of revolving coloured plastic, supposed to be flames, "The Bowl of Light", had in the 1950s been installed in the middle of O'Connell Bridge by Dublin Corporation. Not many Dubliners liked it, and there had been general relief when some students tore out the Bowl and threw it into the River Liffey. Nobody tried to dredge it up, nobody had the gall to try and replace it, and nobody found out who had performed this public service.

When Maurice Hogan, an architecture student and a visitor to my room in the <u>Maison</u>, told me that he had been one of those hurling the Bowl into the river, it was as if I had arrived, on the inside track. I had met Robin Hood.

The food at University City was modestly priced, well within my budget, better than Newtown School but still not very good to eat. I could smell some of what was on offer in cafés and restaurants when cycling around town could see the wonderful produce in street market stalls. When it came to getting a good meal, however, I relied on the people that my parents had asked to "keep an eye on Donal." Those who were asked, it must be said, took that request very seriously. They not only fed me regularly, they became my life tutors in that intermediate year. There was Charles Michelson, a businessman of Rumanian origin with a plan to use Irish radio to advertise gambling (Irish Sweepstakes) in the U.S.A., a plan that took up some time for the employees of the Irish Embassy in Paris. Charles Michelson was a stocky figure, overweight, with dark hair, eyes, and complexion. He cultivated something of a Napoleonic posture (like Rod Steiger), a good scowl and even, sometimes, two fingers hooked into his waistcoat buttons. He couldn't see why I was interested in the Tour de France. "How can you care when it's all fixed by the commercial sponsors?" Helping to look after Donal was perhaps M. Michelson's little bribe to Conor, but it must be said that he took to this role with some enthusiasm. He wanted me to get the point that the world was run by rich people, behind the scenes, that democracy was only a matter of appearance or, to put it more bluntly, a fraud. I took in all this while getting one very good meal every week in his central Paris flat, great food and a little maternal advice from Madame M. I never addressed either of the Michelsons by their first names: my role in that once-a-week little gathering was that of the deferential student, a role that I enjoyed playing almost as much as M. Michelson enjoyed performing as my councillor or Godfather.

Charles Michelson also asked me to check the English translation of a commercial proposal he was putting to the Irish government, a document that included, at one point, the phrase "this procedure is, however, entirely licit." When I suggested to him that the phrase might risk signalling something underhand, or at least dicey, and asked if the word "legal" might not be substituted for "licit", the brusque answer was that licit should stand. I was encouraged to say no more on that point. Charles Michelson at the same time got me an (unpaid) job on the English language service of French radio, on the <u>Avenue des Champs Elysées</u>, thanks to his friend the Minister of Information, Louis Terrenoire. The broadcasters were a little puzzled by my hanging around the studios, but when the Minister's name was mentioned I saw no more of the raised eyebrow.

This was the first year of the French Fifth Republic: Charles De Gaulle was newly President, and there was a feeling of political insecurity, even of danger, in Paris, because of the shadow of the war in Algeria. De Gaulle had come to power with a lot of help from the army in Algeria, and on the Left there was apprehension of a military dictatorship to come.

Critics of the war in Algeria were being harassed, notably including the news magazine, l'Express, which carried material that questioned government policy in Algeria. I remember the street posters, "l'Express est saisi ce matin." How far would the government go? One of the things that I saw in the radio studios was a teleprinter report of more French paratroopers arriving from Algeria at the military airfield in Creil (north of Paris). When I mentioned this to M. Michelson, he seemed neither surprised nor worried: it was just part of the scene. He had flattered me with the tutorial guidance, and I had been intrigued by a peek into his world of business and politics, Balzac for the 20th century.

The next of my life tutors in Paris, Cecilia Gillie, thought Charles Michelson so disreputable a person that she wouldn't even talk about him, which made him even more interesting. She worked for the BBC Overseas Service, her husband Darsie was Paris correspondent for what was then The Manchester Guardian: they both had been in Paris a long time. She was English, he Scottish, the pair of them Brits as seen from this Irish perspective. Cecilia had the accent and the braying delivery that I took to be that of the English upper classes. She assured me of her own modest origins, but she was a Cambridge graduate (Newnham College) and certainly not short of social confidence. As far as she was concerned my Irishness added a little something to the social whirl: "You don't think yourself a citizen of the world, do you? That would be *boring*." She was tickled by the idea that my parents had left her and Darsie in loco parentis while I was in Paris. Darsie did not take to a parental role - no doubt he thought me a young nuisance, all too much around. But Cecilia did in truth become (and remained) a kind of second mother to me.

It was odd that things worked out like that. My own parents weren't particularly close to Cecilia, Darsie was more their friend. Darsie was an intellectual, somewhat aloof, (not only because he was 6 1/2 feet tall) a journalist with a keen interest in archaeology, who took in the broad picture of French culture and politics. Conor had a lot of time for him. Cecilia was about a foot shorter in height, made a lot more noise, and had a perky chin and nose. She was putting on a little weight, made rapid movements, and had lots of energy. My mother didn't much approve of Cecilia. Christine did mention the wild sex life in London during the blitz, and I think Cecilia's braying speech grated on my mother's Irishness.

It had been a surprise to both my parents that Cecilia and Darsie got married (in the 1950s). Conor said very little on the subject: as was often the case, one had to work things out from what he didn't say. He didn't take Cecilia Gillie seriously, hardly talked of her at all. My own perspective on the matter was different: Cecilia took *me* seriously, engaged me in conversation on all sorts of subjects, from life in wartime London to French provincial cooking. The Gillies had an adopted son, of Polish extraction, Stash: when he was around, we shared the position of minors at dinner parties. One of the Gillies' grander friends brought two bottles of fine Claret for dinner on one occasion, and protested, comically (?) at the wine being served to Stash and myself. "Like feeding cream to pigs", was his cutting phrase, a phrase that bonded Stash and

Donal forever. The kitchen was the centre of social action in that household: peeling vegetables or doing the wash-up as conversation roamed. Cecilia was a very good cook: there were fine meals in prospect or to be remembered, the whiff of garlic was never far away. I was an enthusiastic consumer, a hungry boy: Cecilia liked to remember the time that I ate the whole of a Reblochon cheese after dinner, something I certainly couldn't do now.

There was one meal a week for me in the Gillies' Paris apartment, and almost every weekend, a visit to the Gillies' home south of Paris, at Bazoches-sur-le Betz. Bazoches was a nondescript village on a featureless landscape. The Gillies' house had a wonderful assortment of bric-a-brac, strange items of furniture, statues, and all sorts of wonderful local pottery. I loved those country outings almost as much as I did walking around Howth Head in Dublin, a natural beauty spot. There were trips to buy pottery at Courtenay and Montargis, sometimes as far away as Sens, or there were tasks like digging in the heavy clay of the Gillies' garden. In the middle distance you could just see the brightly coloured road building machinery, and just hear the beginning of the <u>Autoroute du Sud</u>, which would eventually take Parisians speeding to the Mediterranean. A little over 10 years later the same <u>Autoroute</u> would take the Gillies too, and their belongings, to the home that they bought for their retirement, in Mirabeau in the Vaucluse, not too far from Aix-en-Provence. When they moved to Provence in 1969 it was partly for the climate but also, Cecilia told me, because she felt by then more at home in France than in England. I wasn't the only migrant around. It is worth emphasis that the person most helpful to me most at the beginning of my migrant trajectory, was the very British, Cecilia Gillie, with her accent, her British upper class social connections and what seemed to me like the coded communication of the establishment.

The third person to be my guide in Paris in that student here, 1958-59, was a man who served as commercial attaché in the Irish Embassy, Miko Fitzgerald. Miko had what sounded to me quite like a British accent, and he had excellent French, also spoken in a British accent. His lovely French wife was of a distinguished diplomatic lineage. They lived in St. Cloud, a very respectable suburb. Miko was also my life tutor in social manners: he didn't lecture me on the subject, nor even mention it, he just demonstrated by example. You work out what your neighbour might want, offer whatever it might be before the other person needs to ask. He and Suzanne talked to me about what I was doing in Paris: they had practical suggestions, useful tips about getting around, places to go, and things to do. In social situations later on in life I have often remembered Miko Fitzgerald, his urbane and inconspicuous assistance, as a model for how one ought to behave: a model coming from the kind of Irishman that some of my compatriots might term a West Brit.

The year that I spent in Paris was not all absorbed by eating at other people's expense, playing bad rugby and hanging around. There was a serious purpose too, not flirting with political science but reading on my own in preparation for the Entrance Scholarships examinations at Trinity College Dublin scheduled for May 1959. History would be my subject, but there was also a general knowledge paper, and an essay on an assigned topic. So it wasn't just a matter of swotting up one's subject, it was also important to look about, do general reading, and try for the rounded approach. I had a game plan here, worked out on an exercise book with a large square format: one square for an hour each day coloured in for each hour of reading, but also (different colour) of visiting the Louvre museum or going out to the theatre or the cinema. There was a cinema at University City, with reasonable prices, films of the <u>avant garde.</u> At the theatre I saw Ionesco's <u>Tueurs Sans Gages</u>, also a play by Albert Camus based on a Dostoevsky story. And if you read Tolstoy, Dostoevsky, Stendhal, Balzac, again you could colour in your squares. I wasn't setting myself an unreasonable target: six hours of reading a day was enough, eight hours a good score. There was a paper on Irish history for the Trinity exam, and I remember reading Lecky's <u>History of Ireland in the 18th Century</u>. There were quite a few peasant rebellions in the latter part of that century: none of them came to much, and I remember being disgusted at the way the rebels seemed always to fire too high, and always lost to the better-trained militia. Some of my own ancestors would have been more likely to be in the militia than among the rebels, but at this time I was with the rebels, against the Brits. Or that's where I thought I was.

The reader could be forgiven a smirk, although a gentle smile would be nicer, at my youthful procedures in preparation for the Trinity exam. But those procedures seem to have worked: when the results came out I was in the top bracket, the third of three Major Entrance Scholars. I was also top for the assigned essay: (something like "Should we try to put a man on the moon?"). My argument, in a nutshell, was that we would only do something worse otherwise. The examiners apparently went to some trouble to check that I hadn't cribbed from Bertrand Russell. "So there," as one might have said in the Newtown School playground. In the oral exam I was able to point out that there had been a line missing in the French text for translation. If things had continued to go on like this I could have become even more insufferable.

Trinity

The year I spent in Trinity College turned out to be another odd interlude, as in Paris I spent most of the time studying for an entrance exam to go elsewhere. This was partly my own fault: on entering, I had decided to take the degree in Economics, a subject that seemed to me to be relevant, up-to-date, might lead to a secure income, as well as being out of reach of my father. I should have remembered what Billy Boggs had been trying to tell me about my mathematics in school. But it wasn't long in economics lectures and readings before I realized that my choice of subject had been a foolish one. History was the subject I had found most enjoyable at Newtown: that's what I really wanted to do. I could have alerted the Trinity authorities to my predicament, the Economics department would have been glad to get rid of me, the historians probably amenable. This however is when my father threw all his weight behind the project that I should now prepare for the scholarship examinations for Cambridge University. Conor said to me that Peterhouse in Cambridge had some excellent historians, starting with the Master,

Herbert Butterfield. The college also had an Irish connection and there was a Catholic link: I would have a good chance. I didn't press Conor on the point, but it was obvious that Trinity College too had its good historians, in the department where he had earned his own doctorate. Conor seemed in no doubt, however, that Cambridge had more historians and some better ones: it was the right place for me.

So my father was pushing me off to England, setting me on the migrant path. Looking back on the matter now I think there were some important things he didn't say. His own marriage was only three years away from rupture: although he couldn't have known that, and although it was chance (and the Congo) that precipitated the break-up, he did know that something messy might not be far away. He also sensed, I think, that it might be comfortable for me to have some geographical distance from him and from Dublin. We have all read our bits of Freud, or got the drift. Whatever Conor's reasons may have been for almost pushing me off to England, I was happy enough at the time to escape from pretending to study Economics, to get back to History, even to take on another entrance examinations campaign. Conor even paid for a tutor to help me prepare for Cambridge, and gave a good deal of his own time over good lunches at a restaurant near to the National Library where I was doing my swotting.

Something that Conor didn't quite say to me at the time, but did leave for me to infer, was that in going to Cambridge I'd be taking on studies that could lead me on, connections in a world beyond what Dublin had to offer: the big league. I had read

Herbert Butterfield's <u>The Whig Interpretation of History</u>, the dissection of ideas of progress. The prospect of study with such people definitely had its appeal: more of an appeal, certainly, than struggling with Paul Samuelson's <u>Economics</u>, our first-year text. The nub of the matter was, I think, that Conor sensed that whatever I might go on to do (journalism was one possible area that we did discuss) it would likely enough take me out of Ireland. He could and would help there. The migrant is thus encouraged to leave which I have always felt was the right decision. And looking around, I wonder how many Irish migrants to Britain were sent on their way by their own families.

I entered Trinity in glory with the scholarship, on the strength of which was allocated a room on the College's front Square. There was no hot water, but the room's previous occupant had been no less than a Count Tolstoy: we never met, but the Count was good enough to leave me the bequest of a chamber pot of elderly urine standing on top of the very tall cupboard. Perhaps this was a Russian aristocratic joke. One of the names on the stairwell was Bill Oddie. My best friend in the economics class was Paddy Lyons, with whom I played quite a lot of cards. Paddy was a substantial person, jowls and just a little corpulence, well dressed in a conservative style, the air of a benevolent bank manager. Paddy lived in England, near Chelmsford. The Lyons family must have been comfortably off: Paddy had his own aeroplane. He invited me to come with him in the plane on a trip to Paris: when I showed up in Chelmsford he looked a bit downcast, said she hadn't been given clearance for Paris (he didn't have enough flying hours) so we would fly to Wolverhampton instead. Even more exotic to me, so off we went, Donal as the navigator with the maps spread out on his knees. The weather being fine, it was not difficult to see the way: we took a tourist route over Southampton water and the Vale of Evesham, and then found Wolverhampton without any problem.

It was when we came to landing that the problems began. Although new to this game I could see that Paddy was coming down too steeply: when we hit the runway, hard, the plane bounced 20 feet back up in the air and my pilot screamed the most commonly used expletive in the English language. He then gunned the motor, and off we went back up again, around we circled. When we came in for the second try there was an ambulance running on one side of the landing strip and a fire engine running on the other side. Paddy took a better angle this time, and the plane came gently down, smiles all around. That evening we went to a bar (no Paris nightclub) in which I drank beer from one of the dirtiest beer glasses I have ever seen. The following day was up and away again: we knew our way and got to Chelmsford, landed properly. There are a couple of footnotes to this narrative: the first is that I met Paddy by chance in Dublin, Grafton Street, some years later, a casual encounter on a centre-city stroll. He knew what I would be thinking about upon seeing his friendly face again. No preamble, his first words: "You know I lost my license over that landing. Somebody in Wolverhampton alerted the people in Chelmsford: they examined the plane, stripped the paint, and found that the struts had been badly cracked. We were held up by the paint." We said goodbye, with an exchange of smiles: there would be no more private aeroplane trips. All's well that ends well. The second footnote is that Paddy Lyons went on to become Professor of Economics at Trinity College. Dublin was where he loved to live: so migration across the Irish Sea isn't all in the same direction. Paddy Lyons was certainly bucking the trend.

The person I saw most of then in Trinity was Robert Buttimore, who had come first in the entrance scholarship examinations. I got in touch with him on the principle that we of the elect should know each other. Butty was small, curly dark hair, with subversive eyes and an air of impudence. He spent a lot of time teaching me philosophy, starting with the Greeks, as he was a Classics student. I must have been telling him something too, but can't remember what, perhaps some modern history and politics. Butty also loved to talk psychology, and to be the analyst. I had at that time a girlfriend, who spent a lot of time with her horse. Our relationship hadn't got very far, and Butty warned me that it never might. "The horse is her father: you'll never win;" and I never did. Butty was a lot of fun, he too made his way to England in due course, became the classics master in Wellington School. I met him at that time with his fair-haired companion, barefoot Anne (later his wife) in rooms they'd rented in a crumbling building in Bloomsbury. The two of them looked to me in the height of bohemian chic: to get into their flat you pressed the bell and an upstairs window was opened, you saw a curly head, and the key was thrown down to you on a string. That, I thought, was the way to live. Butty even had the cheek to warn me of the dangers of promiscuity. I must have glowed green.

Swotting away for Cambridge entrance in History, I didn't even make much of pretence to be studying Economics, never even read much of Samuelson. My thought there was that six weeks of cramming before the end-of-year exam would be enough to get me through and avoid bringing disgrace on the family name. But fate intervened in the form of the upturned bottom of a broken glass bottle, concealed in the long grass of a field near to Howth summit, a field on which I was playing improvised football. I was goalkeeper, took an elegant dive to make my save, my right knee landed on the jagged glass. Six stitches were needed; I lost quite a lot of blood, and sedation was needed to cover the pain. That knocked out two weeks of what could have been Economics swotting. With only four weeks left, my view was that it wasn't worth even trying. So I read not another word of Samuelson. When the exam came I showed up for the first paper but didn't even understand the questions. So I left early and asked our family doctor, who had stitched up my knees, if he could do me a letter for the college authorities, indicating that I wasn't in a position to take those exams. I don't know if Dr. Jessup ever did that, or if he just smiled to himself: he had done his job, and it didn't really matter either way.

The Trinity authorities could with some justification have felt that this phony Economics student was taking them lightly, cocking a snook as he pushed off for Cambridge. I knew that one eminent college figure had strong feelings along these lines: Owen Sheehy Skeffington, my father's cousin and counsellor, had gazed fixedly in my direction during a debating society meeting, while he denounced those who took advantage of Trinity College's facilities while preparing themselves to go to another university. Nobody else looked at me while the peroration went on, and I didn't flinch, feeling that those angry (and hurt?) words were being addressed to my father more than to myself. There were other important people in Trinity who took a more forgiving stance, notable among them Professor F.S.L. Lyons of Trinity's History Department. Lee Lyons could have felt personally about Conor's activity of encouraging me to study history in Cambridge rather than in his own Department. But Lee was of a generation of academics at a time (already) of expanding employment opportunities in higher education, where neither scholars nor their students saw anything wrong in keeping an eye out the window. He was himself to go on to be Professor of History at the University of Kent, Canterbury.

Lyons was one of the two people who interviewed me that year for the Robert Gardiner Scholarship, a juicy little item that Conor had spotted in Trinity's <u>Calendar</u>, a weighty volume that not so many people ever read. The Gardiner was for Trinity students who wanted to study in Cambridge (so far so good) but it stipulated that applicants should be of a landowning family, Church of Ireland in religious observance, and planning to read literature at Cambridge. By a strict reading of the stipulations I shouldn't even have been given an interview, but when I timidly knocked on the door it was opened by a beaming Professor Lyons. Behind him was another historian,

Professor Theo Moody of University College Dublin, also looking amused. When I sat down they told me that they had been delighted to receive my application: nobody had ever applied for a Robert Gardiner Scholarship, the money was mouldering away. Now the assessment panel had at last met, and the two panellists very much welcomed the chance to talk over points of converging interest. That was an opening to the interview. The rest was no more challenging. Whom had I met in Peterhouse? How had I enjoyed the year of study in Paris? I was pleasantly surprised when I was told that the Gardiner was mine: £400 a year for the three years of the B.A. in History. Conor had saved himself some money, and I got a nice pat on the back: off you go to Cambridge, young man, and good luck. Ditching my study (?) of economics was seen by those two historians as a very sensible decision: Moody may have thought that ditching Trinity was another good decision. Lee Lyons was enjoying himself in any case and could, I think, put himself in my place. They both agreed that Cambridge was a good place to study history and Peterhouse an excellent college.

Cambridge

By the time of this altogether comfortable interview I had already been accepted by Peterhouse, awarded not a major scholarship but a modest exhibition of £50 a year. It seemed however to be agreed, tacitly, that the Cambridge exhibition was more of an achievement for me than the Dublin scholarship. Entering from outside made it a bit harder. I was surprised that Cambridge was regarded so highly at the expense of Trinity. Even Owen Sheehy- Skeffington, the

College loyalist and senator, seemed to defer to Cambridge. I had felt a bit uncomfortable about Owen, even before his debating society performance, and sensed his disapproval of what he saw as my easy going manner. He was not only a major figure in Trinity College; he was a national hero of Irish secularism. His letters in the <u>Irish Times</u> were markers in the struggle for freedom of thought in all-too-Catholic Ireland. So it wasn't just that Owen was Conor's father figure, he was well respected by my mother and by my parents' friends as a man who kept up the good fight. I respected Owen too, it took courage to take up the issues that he raised, to confront Catholic hierarchy and established political power. But I did feel myself to be on the sidelines as it was not my struggle and also already took my inner distance from what I saw as local self-righteousness. Blessed are the pure in heart? Maybe, but my own preference was for a little sin, and for people who might see themselves as sinners too.

The student-migrant is on his way now, on the little motorbike that Conor had provided. Getting off the boat at Holyhead, starting the ride toward Cambridge, I was very impressed by the double white lines painted on a road in the middle of nowhere, by the far-reaching and well-endowed authority responsible for those neat and symmetrical lines. I was impressed too by the rain-drops falling from the leaves of chestnut trees along the way, the drops picked out in lowering sunshine. There had been big chestnut trees in the grounds of Newtown School, but I'd not remarked the simple beauty until then. Was I in danger of slipping into the awe of the Percy French song, "Ah Mary, this London's a wonderful sight. The streets do be lit both by day and by night." Perhaps there was a bit of that: the English countryside looked secure, settled, and peaceful. When I got to Birmingham, to stay with my school friend, Dave McEwan, who had a job in the local automotive industry, we talked of family and friends.

London summer

Between Trinity and Cambridge there was summer employment in London and signposts for a migrant. In 1959 the first job was as assistant barman on the top floor of the Queen's Building in Heathrow Airport: this was a position that had been found for me by Valentin Ironmonger of the Irish Embassy in London. Val had ruled out the idea of a job in a London hotel: I'd get to see thing not quite right at my age. He and his wife Sheila put me up for the summer, gave me lots of good tips about London. I would commute from their home in Kew to the airport on my motorbike and would stroll around Kew Gardens or along the river at the weekend. In the bar at the airport there could be as many as three of us to serve very few customers, so there was plenty of time for my seniors to explain the ways that I might defraud the customers. I won't go into detail about those which were trade secrets. There was time to hear my colleagues' life stories. One had sailed with the convoys going to Murmansk in the Second World War: he said that either there was bad weather and you were sick as a dog and would hope to die; or there was good weather and the U-boats were out, which could be your last voyage. I was told such things and offered professional advice in what I would describe as a welcoming spirit to a young Paddy.

Staying in Kew for a couple of months at this time also gave me the chance to see some other things in London: going to Promenade concerts or to pubs. Frank Hetherington shared a flat in Highbury with an English friend, Andrew Lamb. He was the son of Lynton Lamb, the painter and book illustrator, and he knew his own way in the world. Andrew and Frank took me out to a pub in Holborn where Andrew showed me how to move on from drinking Guinness, to try a mixture of mild and bitter ale. It was to be bitter for me from then on when in England. I remember leaving the three of them in their flat with a feeling of baffled admiration: how could anybody live in a place like London? Frank and Andrew did share a passion for village cricket, which they played near to Andrew's parents' place, at Sandon in Essex. So Frank had already found his way into England; he was ahead of me.

The second year of summer work in London was at the Solicitors Law Stationery Society, near Chancery Lane. This time the place for me had been found by George Hetherington, who was the managing director of a printing business in Dublin. The office job at the Stationery Society involved adding up columns of figures, preparing the sums, I was told, for the computer that was to be installed. Not for a trainee to protest, but it did occur to me that the computer, when it came, might do a better and much quicker job than I had managed. But I did get quite quick at the columns, even given my feeble maths, and found it a restful way to pass the day. Apart from doing the sums, the trainee's other job requirement was to listen to our boss's plans for places to go on holiday, or to retire. When he wasn't rambling on, you could think about whatever you fancied at the same time as adding up. What I was thinking about was girls. And this was the summer before I was to go to Cambridge, so I was thinking about the future too. Frank and I did also go to the theatre, together, to see Eugene O'Neill's, "A Long Day's Journey into Night." Why did we choose that play? I'm not sure that we went to any other. As we left the theatre Frank recalled Mary's lines, "Then in the spring something happened to me. Yes, I remember. I fell in love with James Tyrone and was so happy for a time." He had looked down as he spoke, with his own sad smile, a smile we then shared. Our parents' busted marriages, our own childhoods, had all been tied together by the playwright's couple of lines.

CHAPTER 5

Taking Off: Cambridge and Africa

Cambridge: Tutorials, Rugby and New Friends

Dr. Brian Wormald, my tutor in Peterhouse for the first two years of the Bachelor of Arts degree in History, could not have been described as an eloquent man. He habitually wore troubled looks very much that of the middle-level academic, with a cigarette stain on his jacket in the shadow of life's disappointments. I was later to see a photograph of him as a young man, strikingly handsome: not much trace of that was left by 1960. We met for one hour every week, just the two of us, in term time. I would read him the essay I'd done for the week. Then he would set about a vigorous stoking of the coal fire, after which he might have said something about the essay, or about some other subject, or we would have a protracted silence. Maybe it was my own fault: the essay probably wasn't very good, and maybe also he and I had made an awkward start. When awarded the Entrance Exhibition, I had done my bit of special pleading. British students, I argued, would on the strength of Cambridge entrance automatically get financial support from their local authority. An Irish student in the same circumstances got nothing, either from Irish or British public authority. So I had haggled Peterhouse up to making the Exhibition £100 a year.

But when Dr. Wormald learned of my Robert Gardiner Scholarship, the £400 a year that more or less fell out of a tree, he wondered if I might be so good as to return the college its extra £50 a year. I looked circumspect, didn't say anything, and then there was a thunderous stoking of the fire, after which he did say, "I suppose not." We left it at that.

The tutorial system, at this time still gave each undergraduate student an hour alone with their tutor every week, was (I think rightly) seen as the glory of a Cambridge education. Many of my undergraduate peers found it so, as I did particularly in my final year, when Maurice Cowling was my tutor. But with Brian Wormald the weekly meeting was always awkward. One does learn something from silences (Quakers certainly say they do): one has time to wonder why the tutor doesn't speak, after one has read out an essay that could have taken a lot of reading and time to prepare. My considered view on my tutor's silence is that he was a very shy man, disinclined to conversation. When I say that my essays may not have been very good, there were no pointers as to how they might have been improved. The first essay of which, in retrospect, I can say that my tutor's silence couldn't be explained by its poor quality was on the subject of Machiavelli. The relation between The Prince and Machiavelli's other writings, together with what had been written about them, and had really got me going. Before reading out that essay I did apologize as it had taken more time than usual to prepare. After reading it out, more stoking of the fire, then my tutor remarked that often we don't recognize the quality of our own writing. And that was all, either on the essay or on Machiavelli: it left time for the tutor and his pupil to breathe in plenty of smoke.

So a Cambridge education isn't necessarily all that it's cracked up to be. My first reactions to the University were more concentrated on fellow-students then on the fellows. Peterhouse at student level was dominated by boys who came up from public schools, most of them bringing what struck me as a drawling insolence. There were some English friends in my first year, none of them with that drawl. I met them as residents of adjacent rooms in the college lodgings, St. Peter's Terrace or as fellow-players on the college rugby team. Peterhouse is a small college, the smallest in the University: it is also the oldest, as well as having a reputation for right-wing politics and a Catholic inclination. Some colleges were three or four times our size, and in rugby they scored against us in proportion. I don't remember our team ever winning a match. It wasn't collective masochism that drove us on. We got some exercise, some time away from our studies, built up a thirst for the evening after: the Rugby Club dinner, eating and especially drinking too much, plus the hangover the day after that.... There was a street in Cambridge with eight pubs. A runner drank a pint of beer in each of the pubs in short time. I wasn't foolish enough to attempt that, but the idea of that run was an extension of rugby club thinking.

Where Frank Hetherington had made his way into English society by playing village cricket (and made his way back, with equal aplomb, to spend the rest of his life in Ireland) it looked as if I was making my way into Cambridge society by way of the rugby pitch. I was the only Irish player on the Peterhouse team: we were a bit multi-national. Tom Ray was from North Carolina, older and even a bit wiser than the rest of us. He already had a degree; but had never played rugby in his life. He was a neighbour in lodgings, and told us about civil rights agitation, about the Protestant theologian, Reinhold Niebuhr, and was game to have a go at playing rugby. He wasn't very big, but trim, fit, and quite fast on the wing: close-cropped light brown hair, a great smile. "Hang loose, buddy," was his way of saying hello. Tom has since reflected that only a college as small as Peterhouse would have even considered putting him on their rugby team. I could say as much of myself.

Back at St. Peter's Terrace we were even more multi-national than the rugby team. The people I saw most of were an Australian, Brian Somers, Englishmen Keith Goodwin, Paul Le Breton and Martin Staniland and fellow Irishman, Fergal Boland. From Brian Somers I learned about life in Sydney, where the police paid more attention to offences against property than to knife fights and murders among sailors. Brian had a background in student dramatics, but seemed uninterested in carrying that on. He also had a habit of starting the day with half a pint of beer before breakfast. He didn't otherwise drink that much more than the rest of us, but it turned out that he was already on the way to a life in the grip of alcoholism. Brian and I did have a pint or two at the Cross Keys pub across the road from the college, and I took in some of his disenchanted view of the world. But I warmed a lot more to Tom Ray, his sense of fun and of a world of surprises yet to be discovered. There was another American student in that first year at St. Peter's Terrace, who also had a law degree, Jeff Stein. Jeff was very well dressed in a conservative style; he spoke not that much and very carefully, a man of respect.

In Dublin in 1959 I had bought a record of Miles Davis', <u>The Birth of The Cool.</u> Cool was something I desperately wanted to be, to have social poise, then maybe even some sex appeal. The United States of America was my point of reference here: could I hope to have something like the poise of Jeff Stein? In retrospect the answer has to be, probably not, but American friends offered something else, an escape from the public-school status hierarchy of our college and university, from the hegemony of drawling speech. It would have been beyond me to try to imitate that drawl, even had I wanted to do so: my speech pattern was Dublin middle-class, which is to say Irish without sounding too picturesque. I didn't get the feeling of any particular hostility to my Irishness on the part of my fellow-students, heard no Irish "jokes", but at the same time it filtered through that things Irish were held in no great esteem. We were out there, somewhere, upon the borderland: and one didn't look up to the Irish, one looked down at them. The US was another matter in status terms: one could certainly strike a pose of looking down at things American, at the accent or the dress or whatever. But in 1960 that had to look like a silly posture. There was by this time no hiding the fact that the US was the richest and most powerful country in the Western world. One might object to that fact, or poke fun at American ways, but the objection or the fun was always tainted with envy.

Nobody in England, I think, envied the Irish: but the Irish had a joker in their pack in the status game of international hierarchy, in terms of Ireland's own special relationship with the U.S.A. The way we speak English is a part of that special relationship: Dublin middle-class speech isn't so very far from Boston, or from New York (two cities of great importance in the Irish diaspora). I wasn't thinking that out at the time, but there was a dawning awareness on my part, mediated perhaps by a fellow-student. Fergal Boland was, I think, the only other Irish student in Peterhouse. He was also the son of a very eminent diplomat, his father serving at that time as President of the United Nations General Assembly. So Fergal knew a lot about New York, and about American ways. I remember his holding Jeff Stein and Tom Ray at bay with his contention that, although American steaks were bigger then you'd find in Europe, they didn't taste of anything. He could cite the names of swanky restaurants in New York too, places where he had presumably eaten those disappointing steaks. Fergal described his portly father Freddy to me as "a barrel on pins," while he patted his own substantial midriff with the verdict, "all pure muscle."

I don't know how many of our fellow-students gave any thought to the matter of our Irish place in their English world we were beginning to make some English friends, too: Keith Goodwin was a colleague on the college rugby team as well as a Terrace neighbour. He played prop forward, so physically powerful, broad-shouldered, a little less than 6 feet tall, and no paunch whatever: black hair, blue eyes, and a rugged countenance. Keith had been to Tiffin's School, an excellent public school in Surrey with an emphasis on merit rather than social status: he didn't drawl, and his manner was self-deprecating. Mathematics was his subject, and he was a year or two later to remark that his subject changed gear at university level, leaving him struggling to keep up. I could sympathize there: the introduction of algebra in Newtown School had left me floundering many years before. When I asked Keith, recently, to give me his memory of our first meeting, he declared that he had found Fergal and me, Tom Ray and Jeff Stein, to be exotic.

Fergal Boland and I were to share rooms in college in our second and third years: we got on well together despite professional friction between our diplomat fathers and despite both of us being Irish, middle-class Dubliners. He taught me a thing or two: most valuably, he introduced me to the vital concept of the electric blanket, an escape from very cold damp Fenland sleeping. He introduced me to American friends in other Cambridge colleges, notably Gary Hufbauer and Barry Augenbraun. This felt like moving up another notch: Gary had political ambitions, fancied his chances in New Mexico. And Barry was prominent in the Cambridge Union, where he was to be accused of vote-rigging in his campaign. I didn't know him well, but it was something to know even a little of somebody who was, in Cambridge terms, in the headlines. Gary Hufbauer and his wife Caroline were gracious hosts to me on several later occasions. I was invited to Caroline's family's home in La Jolla, California: a very pleasant place on the Pacific Ocean. If Paradise isn't like that, I want my money back. Gary had studied both law and economics: he corrected me on the proposition that economic union in Europe would bring political union thereafter. I should have known better, as a history student. Gary's correction put me in my place: different languages, different histories, were not so easily to be overcome.

In our second Cambridge year (1961-62), Fergal and I had the idea of setting up an Irish club, first in Peterhouse, then inviting in students from other colleges. Whatever possessed us I don't remember, so I'll try to shift the blame to Fergal. He and I were the core members, and then there were some students from Northern Ireland who expressed an interest, came to our first (and last) meetings. What would we do with our club? The whole half-baked project collapsed somewhere between indifference and suspicion. What songs would we sing? Fergal and I did know enough to draw back from suggesting Republican balladry to our Northern colleagues, and they suggested, "The Old Orange Flute." We did have a go at that, but it's a song with a joke to it that works best in a Protestant audience, so we were reminded. We never got to know those Northern Irish students, but they must have been relatively outgoing even to have considered joining an Irish club promoted by two southern Catholics. We seemed unable to disband, but were not anxious to keep it going - North or South, so Fergal and I ruefully withdrew, without another word. It was a club that never happened, an instructive non-event.

We might have taken a cue from George Bernard Shaw's authoritative position on the subject: when Shaw was approached to join the Irish Club in Eaton Square (near the Irish Embassy) in London, he declined, declaring that Irish people in England would do much better to join English clubs, where they would have something distinctive to contribute, and also something to learn. It's not as if we Irish even like each other very much, he said. Shaw knew what he was talking about and he'd lived in England a lot longer than Fergal or me. The Irish Embassy in London has its distinctive position with the Eaton Square club functioning as the Embassy's social outreach. Tim Pat Coogan, an Irish journalist with excellent Republican credentials is reported to have said that the Embassy was promoting the idea that Irish people in England should "integrate, not assimilate." He ventured that emigrants would make up our own minds about what to do in England, come to their own accommodations and go their own pathways, without looking over their shoulders to Eaton Square. The Irish Embassy in London mediated the Republic's economic interests: remittances from Irish people living and working in England. These funds sent back to families in Ireland, have helped not only the families but the whole Irish economy. Irish assimilation in English society could dry up that useful financial stream.

Africa: an Introduction

Something amazing happened to me in 1961, in the summer holidays after my first Cambridge year: my father asked me to join him in Katanga, where he had been posted by the United Nations to direct an operation to end the secession of that province of the newly-created Republic of the Congo. Readers of Conor's To Katanga and Back might even have noticed a reference or two to my presence. My first morning at the residence, the Villa des Roches I jumped into the swimming pool, came to the surface to see an Irish soldier standing over me, with a big smile and what looked like a sub-machine gun. Welcome to the Congo. I was all the family Conor had with him at this time: Christine hadn't wanted to go; Fedelma and Kate hadn't been asked. There was danger in the air: perhaps Conor hadn't wanted his daughters there either. Boys like adventures, so Conor and I (with our Kipling reading behind us) were having a great time, though my father did see to it that I was out of the way before the shooting started. I was only in the Congo for six weeks, but those weeks where to re-orient my thinking and eventual career.

When I got out of the pool at the Villa, I took time to explore the garden. At one point I reached my hand down to get a closer look at something that was moving. A warning shout came from a gardener: "That's a mamba, stand back!" Most of the time in Katanga and elsewhere in the Congo I was well protected by United Nations' personnel, flying about in U.N. aeroplanes or helicopters. The high point was accompanying Conor to North Katanga, a contested area, to see the rebels that were against the Katanga secession. The Cartel Jeunesse, organisers of the breakaway movement from Katanga, was in ethnic terms principally Baluba: in political terms they wanted integration in the Congo. Conor describes our tour vividly in his book. I had talked to some of the people mentioned in Conor's narrative, in particular at some length with Prosper

Mwamba Ilunga, a leader of the movement, and no doubt was indiscreet in expressing my sympathy for his cause. The Belgians in Katanga made it their policy to leave their wives at home when they went to speak to Conor or other United Nations staff: I was like a Belgian wife, giving the game away. Not that it mattered in that case as Conor made no secret of his objective, but thinking over the matter a few days after talking with Prosper, I saw that I might do best in such circumstances by keeping my mouth shut.

I was a lot more discreet in meeting the two Belgian principals of Katanga investment: Prince Albert Edouard de Ligne of the <u>Union Miniere du Haut Katanga</u> and M. Georges Velter of the <u>Sociéte Generale</u> and much else besides. These two plutocrats arrived at the residence in a battered Volkswagen (hats off to the style). The two of them, particularly M. Velter were the charm offensive of aristocracy and big money. The Prince was kind enough to take me aside to give me his view that I was a very fortunate young man to be able to have the experience of being in Katanga. Conor and I made visits to the mission stations driven in another Volkswagen by the charming missionary priest Pere Martin de Wilde, at high speeds along rutted tracks, dodging or over-flying the potholes, as frightening as anything else in Katanga. The aeroplane trips in Conor's company took me to Ruanda and Burundi as well as to the Congo's capital city, Leopoldville. Shuttling back and forth across the Congo River, Leopoldville to Brazzaville, I thought, this beats the study of British constitutional history by quite a considerable distance. An idea of future things to do, future places to go, was already beginning to take shape.

The excitement of this period in Africa was something shared by many observers or students in the early 1960s, the first years of independence. Many young people in Europe or America wanted to help the new African states if they could: so did I, although from what I'd seen in the Congo it wasn't very clear that anything I could do would really make much of a contribution to longer-term development or institutional consolidation. My reflection may have had its small component of altruism, even of generosity, but there was also the consideration of what Africa might do for me. The study of modern history in Cambridge takes the starting date of modernity to be in the late 15th century. While I can see the sense of such a dating now - introducing the origins of bureaucracy and of stable taxation in Europe - as a student it seemed to be out of touch with the modern world. The study of British or of European history was not all boring: there was for example Machiavelli or Thomas Hobbes, but (to borrow some terminology learned later in California) the history of Europe just didn't turn me on.

Africa, on the other hand, with its perils of many kinds, engaged my whole-hearted attention. The study of modern Africa: could a career be in prospect? I wasn't much enjoying my Cambridge studies, and wasn't showing myself too much advantage (a lower second class in Part One). My idea of an escape began to take shape: a possible postgraduate degree in the study of African politics. I don't think I could have been so calculating at this stage, but there was a definite possibility emerging. Was there gold in Africa for me? I would have been shocked if anyone had put such a question to me at the time, but it was becoming clear that I strongly wished to get into the study of contemporary Africa. One took it for granted that in the right circumstances this path could lead on to a career, I thought, in those early fascinating days. If Africa was to be my chosen area of future study, the likely location of future employment would take me far away from Ireland. I was already aware that Britain or the United States was the places where one might get a job, either as a journalist or an academic. Already I was aware that I wanted to leave Ireland as part of my independent trajectory. It was perhaps then that one might put a date on my intention. Leaving Ireland in 1960 to go to Cambridge, I wasn't at all sure of the future, of the places to which I might be going in the longer term, and certainly wasn't thinking of myself as an emigrant.

Conor and the Family in Crisis

The things that happened in 1961 brought the consideration of my own migration into much sharper focus. There was my six weeks in Katanga. And some surrounds parts, including a short trip to what was then Salisbury, Southern Rhodesia. Later that summer, I returned to Ireland: to use my sisters' words, it was then that "the bed fell on father" (with apologies to James Thurber). The UN's attempt to end the Katanga secession by military means went wrong: my father was blamed by the new Secretary General and many UN colleagues. He resigned, spoke out and wrote his story in very memorable words. The people, who wanted to blame Conor for the Katanga operation, notably included the British Prime Minister Harold Macmillan and the Beaverbrook press this helped to make my father quite a celebrity (or notoriety) at the time. Conor had his allies and friends in Britain in the B.B.C. and The Observer, which made for lots of ait time on television. I remember walking in London with Conor at that time, somewhere near Television Centre, when he remarked that all the attention from the media seemed like an illusion of being more real. He wanted to assure me that an illusion was all it was; in reality he was still the same old Conor. I accepted his reassurance, but even at the time my doubts were there. Conor was still my father and our relationship was closer than ever after the Katanga interlude. With the media spotlight on him, a lot of things began to change. I saw my father more than ever as a vulnerable person. It seemed to me that a lot of people were trying to do him harm, some of them with ingratiating smiles as their camouflage. I felt that my duty as a son was to try to give him all the protection I could.

What that meant in practice was, first, to see to it that he took the tranquilisers and other pills that Conor's doctor had prescribed. My father was showing signs of the strain brought on by harassment from a hostile London press, particularly The Daily Express. The strain also in his marriage had reached breaking point. He and Christine announced their amicable separation, and some of the London press chose to portray my mother as the victim. Conor took to speaking in a very loud voice at this time, some of it in good fun, some a little worrying. I thought I could be of some practical help, seeing to it that Conor escaped from the London press mob. Keith Goodwin, my Peterhouse friend, with his Ford Popular became adept at dodging around the narrow streets of central London, always outpacing the pursuers. I also tried to keep an eye on the people my father saw, offering a second opinion on their motives. Elaine (Lady) Greene, Conor's literary agent, later told me that she saw me at the time as a rather frightening figure (as if I took the H.R. Haldeman role, to Conor's Nixon). Elaine was to become a close friend and godmother to our daughter Sarah. At the time, she wore a cautious expression: warm and generous in friendship; she could be cutting too, as a New Yorker. Devoted to her two sons, she liked to hide her own good deeds, which were many. But it was good to know that her first impression of me was as a bristling mastiff. My suspicion was that she might well have been up to no good.

Things were difficult for Conor at this time, but it could have been worse. Walking down Grafton Street in Dublin in 1961 when Conor was still in Katanga I had seen a poster for the evening newspaper, "Hammarskjold killed in African plane crash." I knew that the U.N. Secretary-General had been on the way to see Moise Tshombe in Northern Rhodesia, and that Conor was supposed to have been on the plane with him.

When I bought the paper there was no mention of my father. At that moment I did not know that Hammarskjold had told Conor not to come. In the context of negotiating a U.N. climb-down Conor would have been an embarrassment: the dividend of being an awkward customer...saving your life. My father had been surrounded by Belgian hostility, some of which is chronicled in his book. There had been threats to his life, which he didn't take very seriously. A strange encounter that I had later (1967) on a ship (the <u>Ancerville</u>) going to Senegal is

8. Cambridge Graduation

9. En route from Cambridge to Berkeley, 1963

worth mentioning at this point. A fit-looking British fellow-passenger, with close-cropped hair and a beard, told stories of his military exploits as a mercenary in Africa and offered some useful tips about places to eat en route in Las Palmas. He mentioned among his adventures that he had been in Katanga. "That's where I failed to kill that dreadful man Conor Cruise O'Brien." In idle curiosity I asked him how he had gone about this. "Oh, a bomb by the petrol tank in his car: it didn't go off." I drifted off in search of other company for our voyage. When I mentioned this encounter to Conor a while later in Dublin, he shrugged. "Oh, those mercenaries were always boasting about the terrible things they did. He probably did nothing at all." But the fellow-passenger on that boat had at least succeeded in frightening me.

My mother and my two sisters and I took up new residence at the end of 1961 in a house that George Hetherington had bought in Howth, half a mile downhill from my father's house at the Summit. The house was besieged by press photographers in 1961 when Conor resigned his UN post and was being hounded by the press. Christine had made it very clear that she had no intention of talking to the press. What the papers desperately wanted was to get a photograph of her. Christine had asked all her friends and family not to release any of their photographs. If Conor and Christine were being persecuted by the Brits, the Dublin press observed its own rules of confidentiality. For more than a month, no photo of my mother leaked out. In the trees opposite to Rookstown London press photographers, with their long-range lenses, were ready for the moment that she might show her face at a window, but she did not oblige. My mother did need to get out of the house upon occasion, so we had to improvise. I took her into town, lying on the back seat of the car under a rug, and managed to lose the press pursuers by driving through Trinity College grounds (one little advantage to being an ex-scholar) so she could get her hair done.

That press siege did in its way bring us all together, at least for a time. The siege was in place at both of the Howth residences, although the photographers were in greater number around Rookstown than around Whitewater as they already had plenty of photos of Conor and of Máire MacEntee. Máire had dark eyes, wavy dark hair, and an animated expression. She was vivacious as well as highly intelligent. Conor liked her sense of humour, even when it was at his expense. Máire kindly remembers my activities as a go-between at this time, shuttling between the two houses, and working towards a meeting of all the besieged. I do remember a tense gathering but better tense than none at all, perhaps. Fedelma and Kate and I all had rooms in Rookstown, but we did go back and forth between the houses. My own strong preference was for Whitewater and its magnificent open landscape and sea views, but I think that all three of us children felt that their mother was the parent most in need. Rookstown was a far grander house, with an extensive and well-established garden and a croquet lawn. There was a long gravel drive up to the house, but no view. It was the comfort of suburbia. Fedelma did later say to me that the only thing Conor and Christine agreed about, in the end, was that wonderful Whitewater panoramic view. It hadn't been enough.

The fallout from the separation of our parents may have been advantageous to us children, even if we didn't think so at that time. George certainly took great pains to make us welcome in Rookstown: lots of banter, good food and good cheer. Frank Hetherington however very rarely visited, and when he did, he had to put up with George's man-to-man approach and Christine's barely concealed condescension. I felt for Frank. Lucy, more pointedly, never came. Their mother, Frances, moved from Howth to Clontarf. So, to call Conor and Christine's an amicable separation could have been stretching the meaning of a word, even if one doesn't take the next generation into account. The children, it is true, had been prepared for the rupture of the two marriages, an event that had been telegraphed long in advance. We children could see that our parents were going to be happier now, with George and Máire rather than with each other. Frank and Lucy felt for their mother, and they can't have had much warmth left in their hearts where my mother was concerned.

Máire MacEntee and my father had long been professional colleagues in Ireland's Department of External Affairs, and they had both been on the Irish delegation to the United Nations General Assembly. Máire and Conor had been learning Russian with a Russian family who lived in the Boyne Valley, and there were many trips in that direction for us. We got to know Máire better at this time, the animated conversation, and the intellectual disagreements with Conor, the fun. Máire held her own corner with Conor: not only was she an eminent poet in the Irish language, her family were part of the ruling circle of Fianna Fail, a party that had dominated the politics of the country since independence. Conor had never been a member, as he saw it as much too close to the Catholic Church, and a long way short of progressive in social policy. But I remember a moment, in Katanga, when he pointed out one of the Irish officers with the remark that this officer was a Fianna Fail man, to be contrasted with the more Britain-favouring Irish officers who were part of the tradition of the other main political party, Fine Gael. Fianna Fail, I was given to understand in Katanga, were the salt of the Irish earth: no West Brits they. That was one moment in time when Conor had very little good to say of the British government, but to me his short aside about that Irish officer, a barrel-chested man in the prime of life, gave away a little something about my father's Irishness.

Seen from another vantage point, it had been no small matter for Máire, given her own family background, to come to terms with somebody like my father. Máire was better than my mother at taking on Conor's competitive style. Arrogance isn't quite the right word. While one could recognize with hindsight certain insecurity, he could be imperious with those that he (following Edmund Burke) referred to as his little platoon. Where my mother withdrew inside herself, and sulked, Máire gave as good as she got in the way of take-it-or-leave-it pronouncements. Máire and Conor were a lot happier together; happier than he had been for a long time and life was easier for us, too. Fedelma, Kate and I had been under strain of our own in that crisis year of 1961, changing homes, fending off the press, adjusting to a two-family existence.

Fedelma wrote at the time to John Profumo, expressing her sympathy for a man caught up in political scandal, hotly pursued by the press. He replied with a kind letter. Kate went her mischievous way: she and I niggling at each other: she liked to quote a line from Eugene O'Neill's, <u>A Long Day's Journey into Night</u>, aimed in my direction, "Mother's darling, father's pet, I hate you." The last three words she said three times, with her trademark grin.

Back in Cambridge

It wasn't such desperately bad news to have to go back to Cambridge in the autumn of 1961. Conor's notoriety in the press and on television had its effect in Peterhouse too. Now I was to share rooms in college with Fergal Boland. I think Peterhouse may have wanted me in off the street, away from the press. Herbert Butterfield, the Master, did tell my mother somewhat later how pleased the College had been that I had kept myself away from the press. I had seen enough during those days of siege in Howth to be wary. At one point I had dropped my guard when a member of the press pack had rung the front doorbell. When I answered, he remarked that there were a lot of <u>Daily Express</u> reporters getting cold outside. We exchanged pleasantries on the subject, no more, but the next day the front page of the <u>Daily Mail</u> had my mother and Katanga's Moise Tshombe as "The Lonely Ones," with a word about Donal in Dublin. So the boy was reminded once again to keep his counsel.

Fergal Boland and I got on well. We shared a similar background - Irish with an international flavour: something to keep the public-school condescension in check. We were almost nobs ourselves: there was a bathhouse across the yard from our rooms, and when I had a bath one of the porters saw to it that the <u>Daily Express</u> (his copy, I think) would be there for me to read as I soaked. Fergal told me what it had been like in a Catholic boarding school and what life was like in South Dublin. One economics student in particular, William Keegan, was to become (and has remained) a very good friend. Bill had an animated face, with lots of body language, gestures to reinforce his points. He loved the news, was generous, with the gift of friendship. He and I were to spend a lot of time gossiping in the Marshall Library cafeteria, all the juicy scandal of the Macmillan government's last years. Bill already had his foot in the door at Fleet Street, and he passed along the latest improprieties. In return I would offer him all I knew (which wasn't much) about the C.I.A. in Africa.

We did spend some of our time studying, too, picking our way down the course reading lists, either at the Seeley Library or the University Library. The fellow-student of history with whom I talked most about our readings and lectures was Martin Staniland, who came from Newcastle and spoke with the accent of the North-East. Martin was quite tall, with a head that would have been good on a statue: my sister Kate remarked that he looked like Heathcliff. Martin told me that he felt just as alien as I did from the public-school contingent in college. Charlie Gillett, a fellow-rugby player for a time (he was an athlete, too good for us) came from the North-West of England, and also shared the feeling of alienation from the dominant college culture. I think that each of those two fellow-students felt themselves to be migrants in their way, coming to the South-East of England, the heartland of the ruling class. So the newly-arrived Irish immigrant is reminded that England has its own divisions, most evidently in Cambridge those of region and of social class: good news in a way for the newly-arrived Irish, who were not really part of that. But there's still a difference, I think, between my own case and that of most of my fellow-students in Cambridge. I was coming in from another state, a separate political entity, even if the boundary of separation in empirical reality was quite particularly blurred. I have heard English people remark of the Irish that they're not really foreign. I have also heard Irish people living in England take umbrage at the idea that they could be considered foreigners here. But the age old Irish joke is always there to remind us of our station in a good deal of English opinion.

Times were changing in the very years that I was in Peterhouse. In 1962 the B.B.C. television programme, "That Was the Week That Was," popularised political satire for a mass audience. The people being mocked were in the first instance the Tories of the Harold Macmillan government with their fruity upper-class accents. The mockery was coming from people who often sounded as if they were from a good deal further down the social ladder. The Common Room in Peterhouse was always packed to watch the program: even research students, who wouldn't normally want to be seen in the company of undergraduates, joined the throng, and they laughed with the rest of us. The culture of disrespect, which of course had its generational dimension was, I think, good news for the Irish, certainly so in one small Cambridge college. The Irish are able to freeload on English disrespect; they can be part of the throng. One of my fellow-students in Peterhouse was Michael Howard: Keith Goodwin pointed him out to me in the college's front square, remarking that Howard was a member of the university's Conservative Association, that he wanted to become a Member of Parliament. What a terrible way to spend your youth, such was my lofty thought.

Africa: The Ghana Experience

In the summer vacation of 1962 I went to Accra to join my father and Máire. Conor had been invited by Kwame Nkrumah to become Vice-Chancellor of the University. Ghana may not have been as exciting as the Congo, but it was more attractive in many ways and certainly safer. Keith Goodwin and I had thought of getting a Land Rover to drive there across the Sahara: we were deterred by cost considerations, also by learning that we would have to drive in a convoy in a cloud of dust. You probably could see more of the Sahara from an aeroplane so that's the way we went. We did take the Vice-Chancellor's second car, a small Alfa Romeo, for an excursion into the Ivory Coast, but a car - designed for Italian cities - only just made it back from the rutted and potholed roads of the West African interior. I later took the Vice-Chancellor's Mercedes on a visit to a comely married woman, who had been my tennis partner. Upon leaving her house I managed to get my father's magnificent automobile stuck in a sewage pit. Conor must have been relieved when his son went back to Cambridge.

That summer of 1962 in Ghana was my second introduction to Africa. I was innocently impressed. I met Kwame Nkrumah, a stylish dresser in a white suit that owed a little something to Chairman Mao: he was all charm, asking about my studies, teasing my father. Conor hadn't yet fallen out of favour, with his stubbornness about academic freedom, although he wasn't far from the brink. I went to Akosombo, the new dam and hydro-electric plant, which I found very impressive. The air of economic progress was all about. Much of the local urban bustle was Lorries and buses which sported their own mottos and slogans, often with a religious referent: "In God We Trust," "Jesus Saves," and so on. Nkrumah had style, few doubted, but there were questions around about corruption and about the high-handed treatment of dissent. The state-owned Ghanaian newspapers saw nothing wrong with Osagyefo, as he was called but there was local muttering. On my short stay I had time to be charmed as well as impressed. I wrote a piece for a Cambridge magazine about Ghana which reflected these first impressions.

The Vice-Chancellor's lodge, at the top of the hill on the University campus at Legon (just outside Accra) was a very pleasant place to think over the possibilities of getting into African studies. With that little extra altitude you got as much breeze as might be around, and you weren't that very far from the sea. There was also very good company: Conor and Máire, also Ilsa Yardley, Conor's Secretary and Assistant. Ilsa was blonde, short, blue-eyed, opera-loving, and full of the spirit of life; she gave the world a realistic appraisal, with an eye for the fun of it all. With Keith, she was part of our tennis foursome.

There was also the company of David Brokensha, from the University's anthropology department. David was South African, did his doctorate with Evans-Pritchard at Oxford on a small town in southern Ghana, called Larteh. David was well-tanned, fit, losing some of his brown hair. He communicated his love of Africa (with a special place for people from Larteh) together with his dry humour.

Thomas Hodgkin, Director of the African Studies Institute at the university came to the lodge on the evenings that we were to read Shakespeare, a regular occurrence. Thomas, dishevelled in appearance, a lot of coughing, far-left in politics, with the accent and demeanour of a well-bred Englishman from an old Oxford family He and Conor were two star performers and did not get on particularly well. At the Shakespeare readings he and Conor divided up the best parts between themselves. They were by popular acclaim the best of us: Conor as King Lear, Thomas as the three daughters, and from my bit-part view I'd say that Thomas stole the show. As a young man hoping to embark on a career in African studies, Thomas was of great importance to me. He suggested a route, through his friend Professor David Apter at the University of California, Berkeley. I had been impressed by Apter's <u>Ghana in Transition</u> and Berkeley was certainly well-located, a long way away from family and the great attraction of the San Francisco Bay area. My geography was somewhat lacking, as I dreamed of palm trees as well as girls after Cambridge. The girls at least were to be found.

The way back to Cambridge that summer involved a short stopover in Dakar, Senegal. One heard quite a lot of French spoken in the street; the city had its very attractive Atlantic location, on a promontory along the sea. The island of Gorée had an excellent French restaurant, prime location for a family lunch. So the idea began to take shape: what about this location for post graduate research? One could eat very well, get in a lot of swimming, get to know a lot of stylishly-dressed local people who spoke Wolof and French. So my time in Paris could be put to good future use. I had already heard of the importance of holy men in Senegalese politics, the Muslim <u>marabouts,</u> bastions of the well-established regime. I wondered how they compared to priests in Ireland in those naïve early days.

Final Year in Cambridge

Back in Cambridge things were beginning to look up. This was my last year, and there was the application to do an M.A. in Political Science at Berkeley to point a way ahead: Carry on Migrating might have been my motto at this stage. My studies were also of greater interest. My tutor, Maurice Cowling, seemed actually to enjoy talking, as well as listening. He was a man of dark countenance with high Tory political principles, conservatism in the cynical style of an English Bismarck. Greed, vanity, power, that's what politics was about, he conveyed, so the well-intentioned sentiment in tutorials earned you a curl of the lip. Maurice took Martin Staniland and me together as his last tutorial of the day: we were served whiskey together with our <u>realpolitik</u> which was a great deal more fun than watching Brian Wormald stoke the fire. I really enjoyed Morris Cowling, but I wasn't about to join the Conservative Party. The other good feature of the final year's studies was that "The Anglo-Irish Settlement of 1922" was one of the Special Subjects on offer. Martin did the same subject and we argued it back and forth. At the time, I did regret that the subject dealt with the background to the Irish Free State, but not the Civil War which followed in 1922-23. Some of the people that I interviewed in Dublin, including President Eamon De Valera and especially General Richard Mulcahy, were willing to talk about that nine-month Civil War. That would have made a great research subject, but it was not on offer.

Fergal Boland's American friends were much in evidence in that last Cambridge year, especially the Hufbauers. There was also a Brit, Jonathan Agnew, a friend of Williams Keegan's who planned to study in Berkeley in the coming year. Jonathan did have that drawl, but he somehow disarmed it with his droopy, humorous eyes. He and I were to spend quite a lot of time together in Berkeley the following year. In the Marshall Library I began to read about Africa. The Peterhouse rugby team joined up with Magdalen for a three-match tour in Italy. My most vivid memory of that rugby tour is of a moment in the train going through the Alps when a ticket or passport inspector opened the door to our compartment. We had been sleeping with our socks on, in what wasn't meant to be a sleeping compartment. The smell that hit the nose of that inspector was such that he hastily shut the door. The thought might have occurred to somebody: if you want to move some heroin around, why not try signing up a rugby team?

Peterhouse was reputed in Cambridge for its good food which perhaps obtained for high table only. At the lower tables all that was remarkable was getting two kinds of potatoes with our meal every evening. I remember the blissful discovery of Indian food at the Shalimar restaurant in town, and we did get good pub meals if we cycled out to Grantchester. In the spring and early summer of 1963 I did begin to take more account of the beauties of Cambridge, drinking at the Mill, a pub on the river, punting on the Cam, taking a picnic to the Backs, noticing some of the architecture. But it wasn't until long after graduation that I went into the Fitzwilliam Museum, a building that I'd walked past on the way to breakfast every day in term time for the whole of my first year. A philistine perhaps, but I wasn't an unusual case among students. There were good films at the Arts Club Cinema:. Ingmar Bergman's The Seventh Seal was an outstanding case, but I didn't go all the way with the avant garde. I was so bored and fed up after seeing Antonioni's L'Avventura that I walked across the road into another cinema to see John Wayne and Claudia Cardinale in North to Alaska, a lot more fun. In search of girls, who were still very few in number in Cambridge, I got on my little motorbike and headed for London. There was no satisfactory outcome, even in the big city, a case of my timidity I think.

The application to Berkeley was successful. Pleading indigence, I even got a grant from the university. My result in the final exams for the B.A. in History was an Upper Second Class honours, not brilliant, but enough to qualify for postgraduate research. When I got to Berkeley, and had a glimpse of my file in the university's administration building, the words, "Impossible to Evaluate," were scrawled across the front cover. One of the last things that happened in Peterhouse was an invitation to lunch from Herbert Butterfield. There were eight of us at table, seven graduating students and the Master. In the place of honour, to the Master's right, was a Right Honourable somebody, with Donal next in order of protocol, to his left. Butterfield did talk to me about college matters: I think I was being thanked for not making a show of myself amid all the press investigation in 1961. When I left Cambridge in the summer of 1963, I little thought that England would eventually be my home.

CHAPTER 6

Promised State: California in the Sixties

New Friends and New Ideas

Discovery was expected, as I set out for postgraduate study in Berkeley. The subject of political science would be a refresher after those three years of history, definitely more up-to-date, maybe more relevant. The subject was taken seriously in American universities, and there was a commitment to take on the study of the new states of Asia and Africa. Katanga and Ghana had given me a toe-hold, from there on it was all to learn. The first books on Africa were being produced by mainly American and British scholars with attempts at a relevant theoretical understanding of events and institutions. It was hard to escape the mood of excitement at this time. Political science was only part of the excitement: there was also the more important subject - girls. In Cambridge University, still marked by its monastic origins, female students had been in short supply. It wouldn't be like that in Berkeley, so I had been assured: I already savoured my images of life in California from the cinema.

I went to California in the company of a fellow-student from Peterhouse, Gerry Moore, who had a Harkness Fellowship to study law in Berkeley. Gerry was dapper, carefully dressed, and handsome, with long straight black hair and a bit of that drawl in his speech. He and I weren't close friends, more allies of convenience and in fairness to Gerry it has to be said that the convenience was mostly mine. Gerry had found someone who needed a car driven from New York to San Francisco among his Harkness connections. Freeloading, I became part of the three-driver team. One of us slept on the back seat; one took in the scenery; and the third one drove. That's the kind of thing students did, saving on motels: we drove from coast to coast in three days. My memory is of a great deal of flat, nondescript landscape, whizzing by, and then, quite suddenly after Denver, going up and up to into the Rockies and even a little snow. Coming down again into the Sacramento Valley, we could see big oranges hanging from the trees. You could see what people might have had in mind when they talked of a promised land. And then, when we saw the great bridges of the Bay area, we knew we had arrived. That drive had given us some sense of the geographical dimensions of the United States, also a sense of why the early settlers had kept on heading west.

Gerry Moore and I were to share an apartment in Berkeley for a couple of months, before I moved out to a room of my own, rented from an artistic couple: on the wall were painted some lines from Lorca, "tres golpes de sangre tuvo y se murió de perfil." ("Muerte de Antoñito el Camborio", by Federico García Lorca) The sound of foghorns from San Francisco Bay was a reminder of the sounds I had long been hearing from my bedroom back at home, the sounds of Dublin Bay. I was just a bit homesick. But I was also getting on, reading Jack

Kerouac (On the Road) and Herman Melville (Moby Dick), as well as all that material from the political science course reading lists. One of my fellow-students, Bob Price from Brooklyn, New York, became a close friend, my guide on matters of American football or of the latest in political science. Bob was Jewish, curly brown hair, walked with a spring in his step, and wore shirts with button-down collars. He was also studying African politics, taught that year by an Englishman, Professor Ken Post. Ken had worked especially in Nigeria, but could speak with authority on politics in many other African states. He had a beard, was of impressive bulk: a man with a taste for the theatrical. He acted a part in a Berkeley production of Shakespeare's Coriolanus, but he acted the part of Jack Falstaff most of the time. Going to his lectures was a treat, whether Ken snapping his braces to illustrate the presentational style of (Sir) Roy Welensky in Southern Rhodesia, or giving a one-liner rejoinder to romantic Africanism: "the University of Timbuktu" described as a couple of scruffy mallams under a palm tree Ken wasn't the kind of Englishman I'd seen so much of in Cambridge; he had the speech style of the state-educated insubordinate lower orders. Not that Ken had much time for any politician, the United Kingdom's Labour Party included. What he had seen and studied in Nigeria made him take his distance from some of the optimism of some observers of African politics in the 1950s - of people like Thomas Hodgkin or David Apter.

We had time to talk over all that, with many a pitcher of good cold beer at a pub called Larry Blake's. That was something new for me after Cambridge: tutors were a long way short of anything like friends. With Ken it was possible to engage and talk over the problems of adjustment to American ways, things that a teacher and pupil could share. Ken Post and I were both foreigners in the US. Seen from Larry Blake's, Ireland and England had a great deal in common, more than either country had in common with our new location. I remember a long conversation with Ken after the assassination of John Fitzgerald Kennedy, when we shared a reaction of a something less than bereavement. But we two foreigners would mind our manners and keep our reservations about J.F.K. to ourselves.

I was also beginning to make friends with American students. Bob Price and I attended several of the same classes and we shared scepticism about some of what we were being taught. We also found some of the same things funny: sitting next to each other at lectures, we would poke each other in the ribs from time to time; our silent protest at the orthodoxies of structural functionalism, for example. There was also a French research student in Berkeley who I was to see often, Marc Piault, an anthropologist working on Niger. Marc had something of the looks of Jean-Paul Belmondo: thinning brown hair, a well-tanned face and a boxer's nose. Marc was older than the rest of us: he had served with the French army in Algeria, and he was in love with the cinema. I remember his coming to table one evening with the news that he had just seen a fantastic film, "A Fistful of Dollars," Clint Eastwood - the first of the spaghetti westerns. So Marc not only had style himself, he had accurate recognition of style in others. His wife Colette was also interested in ethnographic cinema, but her principal studies were in socio-linguistics, pretty stylish in itself. Colette had dark hair and eyes, something Greek in her appearance. She told me that Marc had come to her with the good news that he had found somebody in Berkeley who spoke French. I was to spend a lot of time in their inclusive company, Europeans taking a little distance from the American surroundings.

In order to keep myself in physical shape, I turned again to the idea of playing rugby. It had been a little surprising to find that there was a rugby team out there in the far west. I showed up for training with some startlingly large people. It was explained to me that this was Berkeley's football team, keeping fit after the season. Underneath all that padding, American footballers are still seriously big. The training involved some running about, passing backward or forward to yelps of instruction from the coach. Learning the rules of play might have come later: I never got any further than a line-out, jumping next to a much taller opposite number. On the first jump I did manage to get the ball, with the help of a little tug at my adversary's sleeve. He seemed to be puzzled by this outcome, and withdrew to consult with a much smaller player in a huddle. The second time we jumped I got an elbow in the face that almost knocked me out. The smaller player who had been consulted had played scrum half for South African universities: he passed on the correct procedure to deal with the likes of me.

That was the last time I tried to play rugby: not going out in style, but telling myself that rugby-playing was beneath the dignity of a graduate student. It was also less dangerous to keep fit by throwing about an American football with a friend, Stanley Ross, or by playing softball, baseball reduced to something like what we called rounders back in Ireland, with fellow-students. The sporting life was an excuse to get together for a little harmless fun. An alternative to playing rugby was to go to watch Berkeley's football team from the safety of the stands with Bob Price to explain what was going on. Bob had no desire to play the game himself, but he was a real fan. Later, when he became a member of the Berkeley faculty and Professor of Political Science, he volunteered for the invidious role of middle-man between the football coach and the faculty, pleading the case for athletically gifted students who were struggling for pass grades. As he explained the game to me, with the same generosity of intent, it became clear that it looked boring only if you didn't know the rules and couldn't follow the stratagems. I wasn't as much of a fan as Bob, however, and soon drifted off in search of other recreation.

The pursuit of female company came top of the list. There was for a start Eden Lipson, a student with an interest in international relations and a generous way of serving chicken soup to fellow-students in the evening. She had a great social network, maybe in part because she had worked with the college radio station, KPFA. So at her apartment in Parker Street I got to meet many other students, almost all of them American. The various people one met at Eden's place were almost all interested in politics one way or another. Eden herself, the centre of the scene, had a characteristic hoot of laughter to punctuate conversation: she had a matronly aspect but with an attractive face, a good smile. She and I got on very well together, lots of chatter and laughter, but we left it at that. Eden talked quite a lot about her absent flat-mate Rita Abel, a political science student who was at that time on a semi-official student tour of West Africa. Eden showed me some photos of her flat-mate, and told me that Rita would be back in February 1964, a few months away. She didn't need to say put that in your diary, Donal. I later learned from Rita that Eden had talked me up to her, over a table at the Russian Tea Room in New York during the Christmas holidays. So in hindsight it has to be said that Eden did very well in the traditional Jewish role of match-maker.

At this time I was much in company with another young woman, also Jewish, Eleanor Sims from Mills College in Oakland. Eleanor was an officer in her college's United Nations Association, which had got wind of the fact that Conor's son was only a few miles away. So I was invited to talk about the U.N. and Katanga. Mills was a women's college, and I thought that my Cambridge friend Jonathan Agnew might want in on this occasion. So off the two of us went to Mills College, having a look around. I met the investment banker Jonathan recently in London with Cambridge friends, and he remembered this occasion well. Eleanor and I were to spend a lot of time together in the following months. She was very attractive, with the air of having seen something of the world and arched her eyebrows as she smiled. She had a car of her own, a Peugeot 203, and we drove a good deal to the north of San Francisco, up along the Pacific coastline towards the redwood forests. I owe a lot to Eleanor, and we had a very good time together: my shuffling away, in the summer of 1964 still leaves a sad feeling. She graduated from Mills in that year: the Sims family invited me to a dinner in San Francisco at the time of graduation, an occasion when I managed to have a minor accident with her car. I don't think Eleanor's brother trusted me, and he was right. Eleanor went on to become an important authority on Persian 17th century art. She lived in London and New York with her eminent fellow-art historian and Orientalist Ernst Grube, who sadly died in 2011.

Romance

By the spring of 1964 I was already also seeing quite a lot of Eden Lipson's flat-mate Rita Abel. With Eden I had been in the habit of announcing my arrival at the flat by making a rather extravagant chicken noise, call it a loud and frenzied clucking: Donal has come for his soup. One evening, it must have been late February, Rita had returned, not that I knew. When she heard the chicken noise coming up the stairs, her thought was of some weirdo. An embarrassing introduction for us both, and I left as soon as I could. The next time I came there was no chicken noise: but before that I was to see Rita, dressed in style, at a seminar, Poli. Sci. 246B, post-graduate African politics, 5 p.m.

There is a song about it in <u>South Pacific</u>:

> *Some enchanted evening, you may see a stranger.*
> *You may see a stranger, across a crowded room.*

Well, Rita wasn't quite a stranger, we had just met, once, awkwardly, and the seminar room was crowded with twenty or so students. But the word enchanted does get it right. Rita was wearing an orange-yellow linen blouse: I could see her in profile from my seat at the end of the table. Luscious would have summed it up: those lips that body leaning forward over the seminar table, well! To say that this was love at first sight would be wrong. I didn't know this gorgeous creature; but lust at first sight, yes. Rita had plenty of better-placed admirers, such as Eric Levine, the man who had escorted her to the seminar, and I didn't rate my chances. Carl Bergren and Henry Maier were among the other admirers, well-dressed, poised historians who were part of the scene. I was an outsider and a newcomer, but I did have the asset of that well-established connection with Eden Lipson. So if I cut out the chicken noise, maybe some progress might be made: who knew? I didn't really like chicken soup that much, but it was a useful pretext.

Rita and I got to know each other a little better over pitchers of cold beer at a Berkeley student bar called The Steppenwolf, dark, atmospheric. She told me about her childhood in the Bronx, her Jewish but not very religious parents, her brother and sister, the way she kept skinning her knees running forward as a little girl. She also told me about her high school, where she had been a cheerleader and the girlfriend of the captain of the football team. Her parents had moved from the Bronx to Westchester, going up in the world: in the summers she would go to Camp Merriwood in New Hampshire, beautiful surroundings and great outdoor activities for girls.

She had done a B.A. in Political Science, at Elmira College in upstate New York and had spent a year at LSE. When she had told her father she wanted to do a postgraduate degree, he had consented reluctantly, only after her mother, Estelle, with a twinkle had suggested it might be a way of finding a better class of husband.

When I provided my own childhood details, the emphasis was on meagre resources, poverty including picking cinders out of the slag heap at the Mulcahy home in County Sligo. But a Quaker schooling couldn't qualify as all that exotic, could it? So the Paris year and the rugby were rolled out, as well as, of course, my visits to Africa. Here we came to a point of convergence: both of us were postgraduate students of African politics. Rita was a year ahead of me, she already had her Berkeley M.A., was now on the doctoral program. And she had precious resources, like her own hardback copy of James Coleman, <u>Nigeria: the Background to Nationalism</u>. These were markers, as I was falling in love.

We did go to our courses too, in my case to Chalmers Johnson on revolutions, an excellent course in which I failed to excel and to Michael Rogin on groups in American politics (the iron law of oligarchy hidden inside pluralist democracy). Michael was on the left. He and his wife Debbie gave a party which included the singing of some anthems of the left. I remember singing, to Debbie Rogin's delight, of Roddy McCorley going to his death on the bridge at Toome. While I was enough of a fool or a poseur to sing that song learned from a Clancy Brothers record, I was also aware that my own feelings were not in line with most of the other students. Even among graduate students there was a hunger for what was called community: Professor Norman Jacobson taught a fashionable course on the subject. I didn't take that course, wasn't entirely sure what this vogue entailed, but my instinct and small experience told me to stand back. Cambridge colleges and Irish family networks had left me with my own hunger, not for community but for the anonymity of American-style mass higher education.

Eden Lipson's social network brought me into contact with, Walter Tschinkel, a gifted photographer and scientist who became a world authority on ant hills. Joe Pfaff was a stylish cynic and political activist who was eventually busted cultivating large fields of marijuana in the forests of northern California. Willy Cavalla was a very clever undergraduate with a taste for talking about political theory. With Jonathan Agnew I continued to discuss philosophy as well as girls and with Roger Leys, left-wing politics. Paul Sniderman, another Jewish American, kept me up-to-date with the latest trends in political science, together with Bob Price. Even without the female factor, this was turning out to be the best time of my life thus far: excellent classes, the tacos, lots of cold beer, all sorts of different students to talk away the day. Then there was the excellent climate to consider and once you had wheels (or somebody else's wheels) the Pacific coastline and the redwoods were all yours.

Contact with Ireland was maintained by family letters, by discussions with Irish-Americans and by the occasional incident. There was a prominent San Francisco politician, I think his name was O'Halloran, a hero of the local left. And there were conversational signals in Berkeley of the prime place occupied by the Irish in American political life. No Paddy jokes reached my ears in two years. The Kennedys were the talk of the time. I did go once to the Irish Club in San Francisco. I can't remember why, but do remember (absurdly) having been put off by the fact that the members were so completely American. My international driving license recorded the previous license as Irish. When pulled over by traffic police, speeding perhaps, to show my license was to spring from difficulties. One policeman had difficulty believing what he read on the license. "You don't sound Irish," he told me in a recognizably County Kerry lilt. I was able to escape by suggesting that he had been so long away from the country that he'd forgotten how we talked. And I got away with it.

The M.A. in political science (with distinction) duly came my way in 1964, my record over four courses giving a grade-point average good enough to qualify me for the doctoral program: so the application for the following year was completed and accepted. While academic considerations were important to me, and to do a doctorate on something in African politics was exciting, it wasn't nearly as exciting as the prospect of being together with Rita.

A New Relationship and a New Family

The first thing in the meantime was to be introduced to Rita's parents in New York. Estelle, her mother, had been working in the garden: wearing sneakers and working gear, she gave me a wide smile and with open arms announced, "Welcome to Abel's Gables", then gave me a big hug. Nancy and Rita were delighted with this piece of spontaneity. I didn't get the impression, in the following days that Rita's father, Murray, was too delighted at the prospect of what could end up being an Irish son-in-law. Rita told me that his worry was more about what the Jewish family and community might say rather than religious (or ethnic) reservations of his own. Murray and I did keep up appearances well enough that summer, and collusion was to warm into a friendship which got better and better over the years. With Estelle I thought I recognized an immediate sympathy: her inclusive sense of humour, gentle inquiries about my family and education, were an extension of that opening welcome. Rita's mother seemed to me to have something like a spiritual affinity with my own grandfather, Alec Foster, that defiant individuality. She was diminutive in stature, a grand-scale human being.

While staying in New York for the first part of that summer, 1964, there were times when Rita and I could slip away. She took me to meet some of her Elmira College friends, "the swingers", rebels against the small-town conformity of their college days. They certainly impressed me with their sophistication. There was one evening when we crossed New York Harbour on the Staten Island ferry, which included a moment when one of the crew shouted back to whoever was in charge, "Do you see him, Harry?" Then, from the gloom, not a long distance ahead, was the huge shape of a liner, the illuminated letters, FRANCE, high on the superstructure.

Harry must have seen that too. We had left a late night party in Manhattan, had a little breakfast on the island, and came home.

The Abels were going for a family holiday in the Italian Alps later that summer, and I was to head for Ghana at the same time, for what turned out to be my last visit. The political atmosphere was more trying for Conor and for a lot of other people in the country too. <u>Osagyefo</u> Kwame Nkrumah was getting impatient with the idea of opposition. The university had become a target here, the kind of place where all sorts of subversion might be afoot. So Conor as Vice-Chancellor had to try to hold the line, which he did for as long as he could. My sympathies were with him, but I really wasn't thinking that much about Ghanaian politics that summer. There was good swimming at Labadi beach, some tennis, and some evenings of Shakespeare readings. I did also go more than once to George Attoh's bar in town, a place of racial mixing and discreet gossip, with good cold Ghanaian beer. I did talk with Conor about the research I planned to do in Senegal, on Sufi Muslim brotherhood's and politics: he heard me out politely Most of what I was doing in Ghana this time was thinking about the holiday's end, when I would be heading back to Berkeley and to Rita. I wrote many letters, one at least of which has survived with much about love, but also a self-pitying lament about my asthmatic breathing problems. Rita wrote me in return in a more matter-of-fact style, but that didn't put me off. She did say she was looking forward to getting back to Berkeley.

Rita came to Dublin on her way back from the family holiday in Italy and I took her to see some of the beauties of the West of Ireland, including those deep Atlantic inlets. Rita had been most impressed to be collected at the airport by a car with a driver. Stanley McConkey, the Howth taxi driver who used a car without professional marking was taken for my family's chauffeur. I never did anything to set up that impression: Stanley just knew what to do. My mother and George were away at the Edinburgh Festival. Conor and Maire hosted a dinner for us at Whitewater. We headed out west in a family car and enjoyed County Mayo at its bleak best. Our little excursion included a visit to a couple of my family's friends, the bearded artist Grattan Freyer and his French wife Madeleine. Grattan took us for a stroll, leading his aged pale-grey horse. At one point, at a clearing near the top of a small hill, Grattan nonchalantly asked Rita if she'd like a ride. The horse had appeared to be very docile, so, even if it meant riding bareback, something she hadn't done before. Rita said she would; she was always and still is a risk taker. She got on the horse, which promptly jumped a log and threw her off: she landed head-first on-a rock. Grattan, having set up this little ambush, declared himself mortified. A doctor was called, who advised rest, provided sedation, also a small neck-brace. But Rita had to get back to her family in New York, only so much rest was going to be possible. I then flew to New York, where Rita and I did some research-relevant reading in the stacks of Columbia University's library. There was no air-conditioning in the hot late summer weather, so we got down to our scholarly work in swimsuits. Travelling to Columbia on the New York subway, I remember listening with some surprise to Irish-Americans with hurley sticks, talking in Kerry accents as if they had never left home.

Student Revolt and Setting up House

When we got back to Berkeley in September 1964, we walked straight into the first of the big student revolts of the 1960s: the Free Speech Movement. I hadn't noticed anybody being deprived of a right to speak in the previous year on campus, but the student enthusiasm was, for a time, contagious. I was there in the main plaza of the Berkeley campus when Mario Savio climbed onto the police car 20 yards away (taking care to remove his shoes first). Revolutionaries did have some manners is in those days. His words were fine, "of being sick at heart, ready to throw his body on the gears and the levers, bring the machine to a stop." The student audience responded to those words, while the campus police in the marooned car kept their cool. The machine to be brought to a halt was the university itself. There were other issues in the background, U.S. involvement in Vietnam, registration of black voters in the South. But for those students at the demo that day, the issues which mattered most were here on campus. I was ready to be part of the emerging movement, didn't want to look or feel out of place, although there were obstacles ahead. A photograph of me survives, holding a placard, picked up randomly coming onto campus, with the words in big capital letters, "FREEDOM VERSUS FARCE." As I look at that student, still wearing a Harris tweed jacket from the old world, a big grin on his face, it's hard to imagine a sight more ridiculous.

About exactly what could I have been protesting? Students apparently didn't like being considered "just a number" in the college system: no community, no sense of belonging. It was possible to listen with some sympathy to their cry, but my own alignment with the new cause was questionable. "Just a number" was exactly what I wanted to be. Not something to say out loud at that time, even to Rita. She had been at the Port Huron conference of Students for a Democratic Society in1962, knew Tom Hayden and some of the big names of the student left, so I was being pulled along. It was fun to be part of the movement, to sit up with fellow students and a bottle of whiskey to draft a petition, to sing the anthems of protest with the crowd. But when Joan Baez came to Berkeley, sang "We Shall Overcome," and assured us that we were beautiful, I do confess to having found it all a little sick. In the bipolar perspective of the time, I did think myself more of a radical than a fink: not the kind of person to make my signature illegible when signing a protest petition as some fellow graduate students did. But maybe I was unaware (or unwilling to see) that a fink was what I had really become. A fink was career-minded, somebody ready to sell out, who would trade all those ideals for a good safe job. Most of those student ideals weren't really mine, and there was nothing grubby in my eyes about getting paid for what one could do.

What made my stomach turn, at the Joan Baez performance before the student crowd, was the exchange between the singer and the crowd of a feeling of righteousness, an assertion that we were the blessed ones. Were we? I remember the thrill about this time going with Rita to buy our first full set of

10. Free speech demonstration, Berkeley

11. 7 May 1965, Berkeley

12. Leaving New York for life in London

cutlery, at a large discount shop. Those knives and forks and spoons, tokens of the claim to be a household, a self-sufficient unit, seemed to be plucking us out of the student crowd. Then there was going to the Berkeley Co-op to do our week's shopping, including California's beautiful fruit and vegetables. I do remember swordfish steak; it may have been dry and disappointing to eat, but it certainly was exotic. Rita did make Beef Stroganoff, another exotic name, using Campbell's mushroom soup. Most of the time in my bachelor student life, I had eaten at the university cafeteria; for treats there was Woody's where you could get a really good hamburger. Roast chicken home delivered with David Brokensha at his house in the hills, was a regular feature. My second-hand Vespa scooter got me around: its back seat having been damaged under previous ownership, only very good friends would ride pillion.

That had been the regime of my first year in Berkeley: now, between grants and teaching assistants' salaries, we were well enough off. I even had a weekly appearance on television, a programme called "The World's Press," on the San Francisco public broadcasting station, KQED. I would deal with the press from Africa, such of it as the airlines brought to San Francisco. The other panelists on that program were established academics: my inclusion on the panel was passed on from David Brokensha. Professor Chalmers Johnson did Japan, and gave me a lift to the studio. There was even a modest salary. The only audience response to reach me was a letter of protest from a black viewer about "the white racist" claiming to speak for Africa.

Rita and I now had enough resources to buy a car of our own, no less than a white Hillman Minx convertible, second-hand. The roof of this beautiful little car did leak sometimes, but on a good day, with the top down, there wasn't a better way to cross the Golden Gate Bridge. At our little apartment in Parker St, Rita and I had what might have looked like the beginnings of a bourgeois lifestyle. We now had the rudiments of self-sufficiency. Not only that, there was the important fact of the first person plural: "we". As far as excitement went, there was more to me in those two letters that in any amount of student demonstrations: the "we" of two people roundly defeated the larger-scale "we" of Joan Baez's song. The student movement seemed to me to be losing momentum, perhaps necessarily so; impractical to make a routine of climbing onto police cars. David Brokensha, with his experience of South Africa and Ghana, now having taught a while in Berkeley's Anthropology Department, was sympathetic with the students but did use the word "sophomoric" about some of their songs and slogans.

This may just be a graduate student talking from the beginnings of a new household. Quite a few of us, at least for a time, did want to show solidarity with the rebellious undergraduates. There was a time when the University administration outlined a punishment it wanted to impose on some of the rebels. Teaching assistants such as us signed a statement that they too had done whatever it was for which the undergraduates were to be punished. I think it was at around this time that Paul Sniderman and I spent time spinning our whiskey-fuelled words. Did somebody in the university administration just give a jaded smile when they filed our joint letter? I don't know, but we never had a reply. As that university year continued, it was looking more and more as if that defiant letter was also a farewell. It was time to start thinking of one's self.

New Decisions

Enrolled in the University doctoral program, one was committed to take preliminary examinations in a set of political science subjects. Two out of four of the papers were on American politics. Perhaps I hadn't read those requirements at all carefully when I signed up, but even if I had done, the imperative of coming back to Rita trumped all other considerations. What I wanted to do now, though, from the middle of the university year 1964-65, was to get on with research in Africa, rather than be diverted into reading lots of books and articles on US politics. Part of the reason for my reluctance was that I would be starting with a considerable handicap, knowing very little about the United States. The packets of Cheerios in the Co-op were a possible source, with information on four American presidents on the back of each packet as trading cards for children: useful, but the Co-op Cheerios always had the same four presidents. Perhaps that was an omen, a sign to move on.

The University had good reason for requiring those prelims of the doctoral students, equipping candidates with a Berkeley Ph.D. to teach the kind of courses that would be offered in the political science department of any university or college in the United States. But I had not intended to make my career in

America. I was telling myself that it was the research in Africa came first. On the practical side, things were coming more sharply into focus in that second Berkeley year. Professor Michael Crowder, another Englishman with considerable research experience of Nigeria, had arrived to teach African history. As Ken had been my friend and councillor the previous year, Michael was to be as much in the following university year. So it was English coaches, all the way, for this young Irishman in America. Michael Crowder was very neatly dressed for a university teacher, with an accent that sounded to me like that of the comfortably-off London middle classes: gay, at times verging on camp. He had dark carefully combed hair and dark expressive eyes with (like Ken) a taste for theatre.

Michael Crowder was to become a close friend in that Berkeley year and remained a close friend until his early death. Michael was a historian, not a political scientist, and unsentimental: like Ken he denied the romanticism of the African past - one of his references was to "The Bleeding Heart School of African Studies". His own African experience had included British military service and subsequent journalism mostly in Nigeria. Michael had good French, and his seminar brought in French as well as British and American speakers. He had done research on Senegal and encouraged Rita and me in our doctoral projects. He was sympathetic with my reluctance to be delayed by those political science prelims, and suggested the University of London as a place where one could do a doctorate based mainly on research. He had the name of a possible supervisor for me, Professor Ernest Gellner at the London School of Economics, and of some funding at the Institute of Commonwealth Studies. This was beginning to take shape as a possible future move.

The future I wanted however was in the first person plural. So how to turn that trick? Would Rita head off with me to London and an uncertain future? It dawned on me, culpably slowly, that there was only one way to find out. The evening after one of the African studies seminars, given by a French postcolonial administrator, I drove Michael back to his elegant apartment in San Francisco. After a whiskey or two to loosen the tongue, I hesitantly told him that I was thinking of proposing marriage to Rita. His answer was immediate. "If you don't, I will." So it was back into the little car, across the Oakland Bay Bridge, into bed with sleepy Rita. I mumbled the ritual question, got the response (noting the hour and the state of my sobriety) that I had better remember what I had said when I woke in the morning.

Marriage and Departure for London

So there we were, the next day, on a project with dimensions in time and place way beyond the seminar room where I'd started. The first thing was to inform our families, in Dublin, New York and Ghana. I did ask Murray's permission (albeit after the fact) and he seemed touched to have been consulted. Estelle was by this time in hospital, very ill, with a liver ailment. We went to see her in hospital in New York, where I tried to be cheerful, saying how much we looked forward to her coming to Berkeley soon. Estelle's reply was insistent: "No, I won't be". Her terminal verdict was pronounced with sad affection. Conor had already met Rita in Dublin, and while Christine hadn't been in Dublin at that time, she appeared pleased to hear that her son might be settling down.

Then there were the practical questions, when, where, and how? As to when, we were determined that it be as soon as possible. As to where, we talked first of a registry office, but were talked out of that by Professor David Apter, who offered us his beautiful back garden in the Berkeley hills. Find yourselves a preacher, he suggested. Father Gervase Matthew, a distinguished Byzantine scholar from Blackfriers, Oxford and a delightful person, said that he'd be happy to officiate, but then his mother fell ill and he had to go back to England. This got us off the hook, as Gervase had just touched on the embarrassing (to all three of us) requirement that the married couple would undertake to raise their children as Catholics. Rita and I couldn't have gone along with that, and I think that Gervase must have sensed as much. I then thought of a rabbi, but Rita didn't care for that idea.

In the end it was the Reverend Charles McCoy, a Unitarian pastor from the Pacific School of Religion (Berkeley's theology college) who agreed to marry us. This pastor had the right political credentials; he'd been on civil rights marches; he was also a teacher, and wanted us to take three sessions with him where we might explore areas of challenges ahead. The first session dealt with possible religious incompatibility: this we rode through on a secular surfboard. The second session was on sex: one could see that the pastor wasn't much enjoying this, just felt it had to be done. He got down to practical detail for what seemed to me to be a very long time. Rita told me after we left that the tips of my ears had glowed bright red throughout the session, as I stared into the Berkeley hills. The Reverend must have noticed that too: he cancelled the third session, a relief, I think, to all three of us.

So we had a place, we had a preacher and we fixed the date, May 7, 1965. My best man was Michael Crowder. Michael had become a lot more than a teacher, a sort of uncle both to me and to Rita. The three of us had gone together to try skiing, a sport that neither Michael nor I had ever tried before, at Lake Tahoe. While I went in jeans, Michael had bought himself full ski gear in the classy San Francisco department store I. Magnin. He looked magnificent going downhill, poles tucked under the arms, just the sort of thing one might have seen on television. The trouble was that he didn't know how to stop, so he slid all the way to the middle of the car park. I shared the same problem about stopping. My first try, on the papoose (beginner's) slope, was also my last. I slipped gently in the direction of a young woman in pink tights and a fur-trimmed parka whose back was turned, and she bent over just as I got there. An old lecher couldn't have aimed better: so I got a good slap when she got to her feet, and she wasn't at all impressed by my old world apologies and excuses. Michael and I repaired to the bar at the lodge: my best man had been chosen.

Everything seemed to be going smoothly in our little flat when (as in a Raymond Chandler story) the doorbell rang. I opened the door to see two uniformed policemen outside: moment of horror; had the vice squad caught up with us? But these men were grinning: one of them went back to the car and produced an enormous bouquet of flowers, with a note from the Mayor of San Francisco. The Mayor wanted Rita and me to know that he had been contacted by one Alec Foster, who had sent him a cheque for a guinea, with a request that he use the money to get flowers for Donal's fiancée. The Mayor must have spotted the political opportunity here, worth his buying a lot more flowers than Alec's quaint guinea could have covered. A journalist called Rita from the <u>San Francisco Chronicle,</u> to get all the details and an article duly appeared. I hope it was worth a few votes to the Mayor. My grandfather may have been old-fashioned in his choice of currency, but he seems to have had a very good understanding of the realities of city politics in the USA: count a guinea from the old country in votes, and you have a lot of beautiful flowers.

May 7th was, as usual in Berkeley at this time of year, a day of bright sunlight. The Apters' garden looked just right: Andrew and Emily, who were David and Ellie Apters' son and daughter, were our beautiful flower children. An impeccably Trinitarian ceremony went off without a hitch. Michael Crowder remembered to give me the ring at the right time. Rita was resplendent in a pale pink dress that we had bought together in I. Magnin. Legally married, we rang Estelle in hospital, heard her gladness and got her good wishes. Then there was the rest of the business of the day. Family aside, most of the guests at our wedding were fellow-students. Rita had ordered a sheet cake traditionally made for post-football celebrations. Jules Heumann, whose wife Sally was Rita's cousin, had given us 60 bottles of California champagne for this day. J., as he is known, was a San Francisco businessman with a passion for old cars, especially Hispano-Suizas. He and Sally had a house on Twin Peaks with a view of both the bay bridges and the outlet to the Pacific. They hosted a wonderful dinner party for the family the night before the wedding.

David Brokensha, in mid-afternoon of the wedding, brought Africa to the Berkeley hills: jacket off one shoulder in the approved Ghanaian style, a large bottle of gin in one hand, he poured libations into the grass, naming each of our ancestors, as far back as Rita or I had been able to remember. David remembered every one, as each of them got their little snorter. His performance was a show-stopper, and at this point I did have some sympathy for the Reverend McCoy. The pastor had gone out of his way to help us: was this a way to thank him, in a cluster of secularists or pagans? But he would have known his Berkeley: he can't have been that surprised. Rita and I thanked him with a long- playing record of the Missa Luba, Congolese Christian chants.

We knew we had to leave when one of our undergraduate student-barmen came to us with the news that they were about to open their last bottle. It wasn't a huge party, so our thirsty friends must have accounted for more than a bottle each. So Rita and I climbed into the Ford Mustang that Paul Sniderman had lent us for our honeymoon, departing with a spurt of gravel that may have given him a troubling moment. Our destination was Timber Cove Inn, a leisurely few hours' drive north along the Pacific Coast. When we got to the Inn we were on a special deal for honeymooners, including half a bottle of champagne on the house: we did feel we had to polish that off too. Our honeymoon location was poised on a bluff looking down at the ocean you could hear the sound of the surf. A lovely spot, but Rita and I had allocated ourselves only a single day of honeymoon. Having dragged our families from New York, Accra and Dublin to come to the wedding, we felt we had to get back to see them before they left.

When we got back to Berkeley it was to hear tales of what must have been a very good party. At an evening in San Francisco, Conor had read out the complete poems of W. B. Yeats to three adoring divorcees. David Brokensha discovered the next day that another divorcee had slipped a credit card into his pocket - a Bay-area way of saying, can't we be in touch? I don't know what else happened at that party, but perhaps it was just as well that we had come back. Paul Sniderman must have been glad to see his car again, and our families could see some of the newly married couple. Christine George, Conor and Maire had hosted Fedelma and Kate's travel, so Christine did not attend for cost reasons. It was good to see them all again, an extension of the gathering in the Berkeley hills, to talk over our plans for the future, when we'd be heading back east.

Michael Crowder had been councillor to our future plans to go to London and then to West Africa. He had the right connections, knew the routes and wrote the right letters of recommendation. In order to fit the specifications for the Junior Research Fellowship at the Institute of Commonwealth

Studies, I declared that my field research interest was in a comparative study of Senegal and Sierra Leone. Professor Kenneth Robinson, Director of the Institute, had written very perceptively on Senegalese politics, but there was no hiding the fact that officially Francophone Senegal was outside the Commonwealth. The little subterfuge about Sierra Leone was enough to fit me into the Institute.

Looking back on all that now, I think there is a larger question for me to answer. Why all that urgency about getting out of California? Was it really, as I thought at the time, just a matter of getting on with that field research? There was a latent consideration, lurking in the background, of the place where one imagined one's future might lie, the place where one imagined oneself settling down. Rita and I were doing well enough in Berkeley: I could with a little effort have boned up on my American history and politics, passed those prelims and then done the field research, the path to becoming professor somewhere in the USA. But America wasn't my career objective, for the unprofessional reason that it would have been entailed too radical a separation from my family, my mother and sisters especially. Conor would catch up with us wherever. Christine really didn't like to travel long distances. If her son were to end up settling in Britain, that would not be very good news, but better at least than having him all the way across the Atlantic. There were also my own considerations at the time: the Free Speech Movement was beginning to look like a time-consuming bore, diverting us from our studies. Further back in my mind was the idea that I would feel more at home "back" in England.

This was all very well for me, but what about my American wife? The same considerations of separation from family applied to Rita too. Each of us was moving out of the family by the fact of our marriage, but for Rita it would be not only out, also away. It was fortunate for me that in those days the balance of power in gender politics was still weighted towards male decisions. I had blithe confidence that we would do well in London, a big enough place to accommodate two separate careers. Roll the clock on another 20 years, Rita might have dug in her heels, I would have stopped joking about Cheerio packets, be writing these words somewhere in the USA Writing now in Dorset, England, I confess to being very pleased that things worked out this way.

Having said our goodbyes to fellow-students, teachers, and friends, we made our way to New York, and it wasn't long after we got there that Rita's mother died. Murray extended an arm to pull me into the little family huddle outside the hospital, of grief and tears: Murray, Jerry, Rita, Nancy...and Donal. Murray's arm was a generous gesture, in line with Estelle's welcome to Abel's gables, but after some minutes in the huddle I gently moved away. Their grief was of an intensity, based on a lifetime of memories, that left me feeling the need to respect the gap between their grief and my own as a newcomer. The weeks that followed, in the Abel household continued the grieving. There was also some jockeying for position around Murray. Murray used what energy he had to fend off the women who seemed to see themselves taking what had been Estelle's place: most of the day the poor man just moped. After a couple of weeks of this I took on myself a camp-counsellor role, no doubt prodded in this by Rita. To get Murray out of the house we went to the movies as often as possible: I remember "Genghis Khan" with Omar Sharif, but anything that allowed for a little chat afterwards would do. It was from this time that Murray and I became friends: he could see what I was trying to do, and he even managed an occasional smile.

Rita and I sailed from New York on the <u>Maasdam</u> (Holland-America Line), with our books, papers, note-cards, wedding presents and other belongings. We had enough possessions by this time to make it necessary that we go by sea, and it was much cheaper than flying. One prize in particular was the magical Sudanese painting of a crocodile which had been Michael's wedding gift. It was a very long water based painting on poor paper which had been mounted on a plywood backing. We had to have the crocodile sawed in half for transit. We put him back together, none the worse, and mounted him on the wall, when we got a home of our own, in London where he still presides over our lives.

The sea voyage was, as they say, uneventful, if you discount Kevin Casey and The Maasdam Trio, singing over and over again of watching the sun go down on Galway Bay; or of it being spring again, so we'd sing again, of tulips in Amsterdam. Our arrival in Galway, after seven days of such entertainment, coincided with a major official commotion: big cars for Catholic eminences, several cardinals had come to officiate at the installation of a bust of John Fitzgerald Kennedy in a square named for the former American president in the centre of town. My mother and George had driven to greet us and we enjoyed a champagne picnic on the way back to Dublin. This was Rita's first meeting with either Christine or George: the picnic went well, and we went back home for a family summer. Then we packed up again in September to head for our new lives in London: we had saved enough money, from our California salaries, to last more than two years. We also had each other.

CHAPTER 7

Quest for Knowledge: Research in London, Paris, Dakar and Touba

Research Ideas and new Academic Links

Among the things I learned from Berkeley political scientists was their sense of the researcher's nobility of purpose, out there on the frontier of globally-expanding political study. There had been studies of African politics in towns, of movements and parties, but not that much was known of politics in small towns and villages. Many felt that the very idea of politics in rural Africa was simply misplaced: this was where tradition ruled, the traditional terrain of anthropologists. The graduate students of political science in Berkeley had no time for such relegation. We thought ourselves at a moment of opportunity, when we could learn and borrow from anthropologists and historians, while we opened up a new field, the study of post-independence politics. So there was opportunity, although still only in general terms: we'd identified what was little known. How to get inside that broad perspective, to focus on a research subject of a manageable size?

The pursuit of knowledge was a grand thing, the pursuit of personal advantage hidden within. The choice of a research subject might have been expected to focus one's attention on the issues radiating out from the simple question, "What's in it for me?" But hand on heart I can say that, as I considered things in 1965, the grand generality still did a good job hiding the personal considerations. I knew however that the choice of a research subject was significant: if one did the research thoroughly one would, for a time, know more on that subject than anybody else. This was a route to intellectual self-sufficiency, narrowly defined. Beyond that were the material considerations: the award of a doctorate, a Ph.D., the academic's trade union card, as my supervisor in London was later to put it. Then there would be better opportunities for employment (especially in those days), material security to complement the intellectual. But in 1965 such things were beyond the horizon. I was looking for a subject to make my own, a place where I could snarl, like the bad guy in a western, "Get off my land!"

The Sufi Muslims of Senegal became my focus for a range of reasons. Consideration of their political situation became central to my academic career. The first point of attraction was that one would be dealing with religious communities, with believers, reaching people whose organization owed little or nothing to European principles. Quaker schooling had given me a taste for talk with believers. The second point was speculative, again relating back to Ireland. The leadership of Senegal's Sufi communities, <u>marabouts</u> had established their hierarchies in parallel with the structures of the colonial state.

Was there a possible comparison here with the role of Christian monasteries in medieval Ireland? The colonised could withdraw to their communities of belief. The third point of attraction has already been mentioned, that Senegal was an ex-French colony (independent in 1960): the archives and official documentation would be in French. My year in Paris would stand me in good stead. The fourth point was that this was a subject for political study that demanded historical treatment: I may not have enjoyed Cambridge much, but the historian's approach to politics wasn't so easily shaken off. A final point was the situation of Senegal's marabouts in terms of nationalist politics: were these the lackeys of colonialism, or the defenders of their own turf? Adding these points together, I knew that I had a subject, although exactly how to proceed was something that remained to be decided.

The first academic to look over my file at the London School of Economics, at the induction interview, was the fierce and famous Professor Lucy Mair of the Anthropology Department. She knew exactly how I should proceed: my subject was anthropology, and she more than hinted that she herself should be my supervisor. Dismay and panic were mine: she looked as though she was used to getting her way, but I certainly didn't look forward to years ahead under her supervision. My interviewer was slightly wizened, domineering, an authority on witchcraft: how could I escape? In desperation I said that the study I had in mind was not anthropological, and that Professor Ernest Gellner of the Sociology Department was the supervisor I had in mind. Michael Crowder back in Berkeley had suggested Gellner on the basis of his Moroccan study, Saints

<u>of the Atlas</u>, also as an intellectual of wide reach. It's also worth remarking that in Berkeley we budding political scientists had looked on anthropologists as yesterday's people, with their colonial taint. But there and then in London, Lucy Mair had little regard for my suggestion. "Professor Gellner is a very busy man. He won't have time for you." So I walked out of her office, straight to Gellner's office, knocked on the door.

When told to come in, I hardly let the professor get in a word. My line was that I knew how busy he was; promised not to take up his time, that all I wanted was that he sign my forms, let me get on with my research. Gellner was a small man with a large head, dark curly hair, and dark piercing eyes. With a half-smile he raised his eyebrows and asked who I'd been talking to: "I get paid as a supervisor." When I named my source, Gellner's smile broadened: I was in.

Ernest Gellner proved to be an excellent supervisor, but it seemed that there wasn't that much he could do for me at this stage. The thrilling truth was that in research terms I really was on my own: there were background books to be read, plans to be made before going on to Paris and then Senegal, funds to be raised. Rita and I learned a little Wolof with the help of some Gambian and Senegalese students, and David Dalby of the Africa (languages) Department in the School of Oriental and African Studies. I won an award from the Social Science Research Council to finance the research, with Gellner's reference, but was to be struck off when a zealous diplomat at the British Embassy in Dakar later pointed out to the funding body that I was a national of the Irish Republic, ineligible therefore for an award from the British Social Science Research Council. At the time that looked to me like an injustice: Irish nationals could vote in British elections, were entitled to British social security, so why not to research awards also, if they were registered at British universities? But the Irish anomaly wouldn't stretch that far. My supervisor's recourse, when I pulled the alarm cord, was to contact a friend of his in the Overseas Development Administration, pleading the value of my research for British interests in Senegal and the Gambia. That got me some British money, and there were still the savings from California: we could proceed.

I wasn't yet quite aware of being in the process of becoming a little bit British, with some bumps and scrapes along the way. The Junior Research Fellowship at the Institute of Commonwealth Studies gave me entry to an excellent library in Russell Square, a pleasant place to read, with a carpeted common room well-appointed for morning coffee and afternoon tea. Mr. Savage, the Institute's porter, was the man in charge: mostly bald, some silver whiskers still on either side, red-faced, waistcoat and shirtsleeves, dispensed tea from a very large urn in proper cups and saucers, milk in a jug, biscuits on a plate, this was the correct ritual. Mr. Savage wasn't a social scientist, but he knew in his bones that ritual creates community, when it is correctly performed.

There was room in the Institute's community for young scholars from Ireland as well as the Commonwealth. Richard Rathbone was the established figure already: English, tall, with a very large body, well-dressed, a man who knew his way around. Richard was also a lot of fun, a good mimic and thoroughly up-to-date. His research was on the last British governor of the Gold Coast, Sir Charles Arden-Clarke, the man who saw to it that the colony became independent, as Ghana, in 1957. He explained the ways in which the Governor had smoothed the path to power for Kwame Nkrumah, saw off the opposition, made sure that he became Ghana's first president. Richard and I had plenty to talk about, and we became good friends: he was my principal guide to academic London. Stanley Trapido, another Junior Fellow, introduced me to key South African concepts, the polarity of <u>hensoppers</u> and <u>bittereinders</u> at the end of the Boer war, and thereafter.

Settling into Life in London

My father was occasionally around while we were in London. His arrival brought some very good meals, great talk and cheer, a ringside seat for the current controversies. Through Conor we knew (Lady) Elaine Greene, his literary agent who became very important in our lives. We also knew Ilsa Yardley, who had been Conor's secretary at the University of Ghana. Ilsa and her husband Maurice gave very generous high-profile parties, featuring "goldfish bowls" of whisky: very good news for thirsty students, lots to eat and drink, as well as a look at literary London. We heard our share of disparaging Irish jokes, from people who would never have made an anti-Semitic or other racist remark. Two years later the Provisional I.R.A. began their bombing campaign. One of their casualties was the Irish joke: no longer was a figure of fun, Paddy dangerous now. So for that at least, thank you, Gerry Adams.

My use of the family surname went through transition during these years in London. In Newtown School I had been plain Donal O'Brien. Perhaps those humane Quaker teachers in Waterford wanted to shield me from the teasing that might have preyed upon a double-barrelled surname. Although Conor remained a celebrity, I still wasn't sure that I wanted to be immediately identifiable as Conor's son (the first item of conversation being "How's your father?"). By this time I had taken stock of the fact that on my birth-certificate, my surname was Cruise-O'Brien. My parents must have gone along with that at the time (Fedelma very plausibly supposes that drink could have been a factor), but two decades later Conor would have none of the hyphen, an English imposition on Irish usage. I wasn't fussed about the hyphen, more convenient for filling in forms, but the Cruise could have been too tight a bond to my father as a well-known public figure. I was proud of him, of his courage as well as his intellectual gifts, loved him for his foibles, the fun that he brought with him, but my hankering for a space of my own was certainly apparent. There was however no hiding the obvious: in a bar, a member of faculty at the L.S.E. with a broad smile put it to me in a nutshell: "always use the full Cruise, Donal." He didn't spell out his reasoning, but I would be blamed by some for being Conor's son whatever my surname. Cruise O'Brien had a nice ring to it, and its historic origin: play it right, it's a name that could give you a little breathing space.

Most of what I was doing in London was settling down with Rita, adjusting to life in a one-room flat over the Angel Bookshop in Islington High Street. We slept on a leatherette sofa-bed that tilted the occupants towards the wall: no danger of falling out, but some discomfort if you got caught between the hard seats. A burglar alarm across the road went off either in the rain or at the weekends, when nobody bothered to come turn it off. Our next-door neighbours, Lee and Frank, a gay partnership in the antiques trade, helped us move in. At one point, manoeuvring a cupboard round a corner on the stairs, Lee told Richard Rathbone, who was also helping: "You can turn around now, it's legal." We did our shopping at Chapel Market across the road: basic root vegetables and English fruit, nothing out of season. Here we discovered fried plantains, delicious with ginger and garlic. Sainsbury's was right next door to the market, so we had everything within easy reach.

A near-disaster helped us to grow up a little. Rita was rushed by ambulance to Hackney Hospital, had an emergency operation for what we were later told was a cervical ectopic pregnancy. Seven pints of blood were used in transfusion, and Rita was packed full of dry ice to avoid a hysterectomy. Mr. Woolf, the surgeon, told me that the ice was his idea, on reading Rita's age (24) on the tag around her wrist. He decided not to do a hysterectomy, the standard procedure in such cases. He also told me that it might not work; he would then have to proceed to save her life. I was to ring when the dressing was removed. It was from the Rathbones' flat in Southampton Row that I made that call, asking his wife Frances to pull up a chair behind me. But the news was good, the daring procedure had worked, Rita would be fine. Tony Woolf was the very best of the National Health Service, one of London's foremost gynaecologist's, a risk-taker to preserve child-bearing: from his Harley Street consultancy to his work in Hackney, which he called "End of the World, E9." Handsome, dashing, dark hair: may his name be praised forever.

Our point of contact with teachers and other research students was the L.S.E. Sociology of Development seminar: Professors Ernest Gellner and Ron Dore, Dr. Emanuel De Kadt, made up the teaching panel. Each one of them was to become a life-long friend. Rita and I, with our Berkeley background, may have been seen as snobs by most of the students. We had done our share of political sociology starting with Max Weber, the exciting American idea of a world mapped according to structure and function rather than European-modelled institutions. This was a new map in which Africa had an important and intriguing place. One might be a dissident, but could take pride in knowing one's share of Talcott Parsons, Robert Merton, David Easton, Gabriel Almond, some of the major figures in American social and political science. As doctoral students we also missed out on the Beatles and the Rolling Stones, weren't really much of a part of swinging London in the Sixties. We were very serious, probably more than a little unbearable. There was a moment, in the Common Room of the Institute of Commonwealth Studies that I was to recall to my own students in later years. News had reached us of the military coup in Nigeria, January 1966, and the consensus of our little group of not very learned scholars was that the new regime couldn't be any worse than the corrupt one that had just been overthrown. Idealistic young military officers were involved, but, whatever their intentions, the consequences of their actions were to include the huge loss of life of the failed Biafra secession, 1967-71.

Research in Paris

Paris was the next stop, in April, the beginning of real research for both of us. Here I worked on colonial Senegal in the Archives d'Outre Mer, and the past holdings of Senegalese newspapers in the Bibliothèque Nationale. We were staying in the maid's room (chambre de bonne) attached to the Gillies' flat in the Rue Casimir Perrier, 7e arrondissement. It wasn't a big room; one of us had to stand outside the door so the other could put down the camp bed and then jump in every evening. While it wasn't very comfortable, it was under the eaves of the roof of the building, and if you got out on the little iron balcony you had a very good view of the Eiffel Tower. Cecilia took us in hand, insisting that we couldn't possibly go to Senegal without introductions from significant officials in Paris. She had a friend, Sylvain Lourie, then with UNESCO but previously a French diplomat, who did see us and provided introductions which were to lead, in my case, straight down the postcolonial chain of command to the young man in Touba who was to ensure the success of my research. The other big moment for me in Paris was an interview with Professor Georges Balandier, eminent anthropologist and the leading figure of French African studies. Balandier was a small man, radiating intelligence and practicality. He heard me out on my project to study Sufi Muslims and politics in Senegal, put his head on one side, suggested that I do just the Mouride brotherhood. "They are the most interesting ones," he said. Balandier knew Senegal, about which he had written well, and his advice made me re-focus the research. Professor Louis Brenner, later my colleague and friend at the School of Oriental and African Studies, said of that Paris moment, "He made your career."

Rita was getting on with her own research, on the French people living in Senegal after independence, building up her confidence in the use of spoken French. Our French friends from Berkeley, Marc and Colette Piault, were now back in Paris, and they were very generous with hospitality as well as gentle advice for the two of us. They had their own experience of trying to adjust to a foreign-language environment: so they didn't correct Rita when she spoke. They let her keep going, and kept up the conversation. One of their friends was the film maker and anthropologist Jean Rouch who joined us at Colette's parents' elegant family home in Normandy for the long Easter weekend. Rouch had been living with surfies in Australia, and he was a gifted storyteller. A "stomper" is a big wave that falls right down on top of you. Rita commented later that it was with the Piaults but that she concluded that she really could get away with speaking French. She never looked back. To acquaint her with my past privations I took her to the student restaurant in the Cité Universitaire: she was witness to the toughest and most inedible giant artichoke. But that was only once. For the most part it was good French fast food in the cafés, or very good French food with friends.

Arriving in Senegal

We sailed for Dakar from Marseille in September on the Ancerville, with the car, a red Volkswagen Beetle, that Rita's father, had bought as a belated wedding present. We left port in a howling offshore gale, a Mistral, and our boat had to be manoeuvred out by two tugs. The Ancerville kept as close as possible to the coast of France, then Spain, so we had the chance to see a lot of lamentable-looking high rise hotels and flats along the way. We were in 3rd class, with mostly African fellow-passengers.

When we arrived in Dakar, September 1966, the shoreline was recognizable as the landscape/seascape we had seen represented in many historical prints. A few modest skyscrapers had been added. We came at the time of year locally known as the hivernage, a steamy season very occasionally relieved by rainfall. The mosquitoes were very active. Our first accommodation, arranged from Paris, was in a low building provided for transient researchers in a tropical garden at the Institut Fondamental (previously, Français) d'Afrique Noire (IFAN).The rooms were placed under the overhang of some very old trees, next to the Institute's Museum. There was no air-conditioning and no screens, perhaps the Institute's authorities wanted to be sure that the researchers' passage not be prolonged. We followed the advice of a slightly more experienced colleague, a black American scholar who told us: "Get yourselves a very big aerosol can of insecticide, have a cold shower, spray all around the room, and jump into bed." That way you might one hour's sleep at a time before you were sweating enough to have mosquitoes all over you again. In that case you got up, had another cold shower, did another spray-about, tried to get a little more sleep: so on, and on, through the night.

After three nights of this Rita came to the rescue. Interested in urban development, she knew about housing estates run by the Societé Immobilière du Cap Vert, S.I.C.A.P. At the head office she enquired if there might be anything available for rent. "Why no," said the front-desk official, "our housing is only for long-term Senegalese occupancy." But there was a young man at the back of the room, who overheard the request and came forward to have a word in confidence. He had an uncle with a house in S.I.C.A.P.-Baobabs, who might be able to help us.

The deal was swiftly done: we moved into a small concrete house, with coloured light bulbs, a small bar in the hall. We soon discovered that this had been a house of ill repute, when clients came knocking on the windows late at night. Hygiene clearly hadn't been a priority for our predecessors: there was an army of cockroaches all over the house. The first precaution, at night, was to reach your hand into the room, turn on the light, and give the roaches time to move off. then enter. We procured a noxious chemical powder to scatter all about the floors, the yard, the corners and crevices: then bleach to wash down the tables, chairs, cupboards. We were in the yard in our swimsuits, in full clean-up mode, when I saw a nose coming round the corner, a large bead of perspiration dropping from the end. "Je suis Claude Meillassoux," our visitor announced, and at this point I felt that we really had arrived in Senegal. A distinguished Marxist anthropologist, with a great reputation in Paris, had come to see us in what had just ceased to be squalor.

S.I.C.A.P. housing had been provided to offer low-cost housing to junior civil servants in Dakar. There wasn't another white face to be seen on the estate, where our neighbours greeted us with amused courtesy. What we were doing was moving into the grey economy. We were comfortably installed: eventually there was real mosquito netting and best of all there was an air-conditioner in the bedroom. At last we could get a good night's sleep. There were several mango trees in our small front yard and a bougainvillea hedge. The cockroaches had been put to rout, you could walk into a room at night without even turning the light on first.

Research in Dakar and Touba

It was time, then, to get down to our studies. We both began at the National Archives. For me this was a treasure house. French colonial authority had been keeping a close eye on the Mouride brotherhood from the beginning, a time of origin shared by colony and brotherhood, the late 19th century. There were plenty of inside assessments, from the political police of Renseignements Généraux, of the reliability of individual holy men, as well as some candid-looking policy statements. My detailed reading was to prove a significant resource to me when the research took me inland to Touba, where my informants would ask me what was said in the Dakar Archives about them or their forefathers. Those Archives were impeccably organized: you could see anything up to 1940 and quite a bit thereafter. In Paris the colonial archives closed in

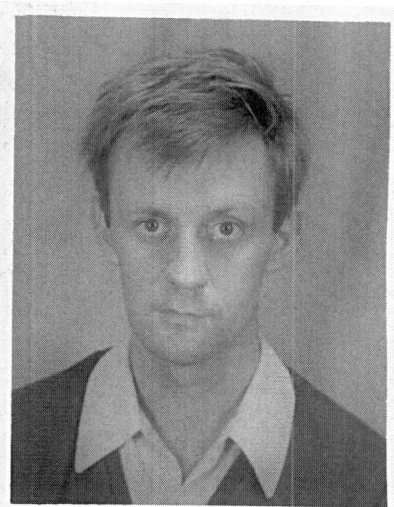

13. Young researchers en route to Senegal, 1967

14. Relaxing in Touba

15. Interviewing Mourides

16. Receiving the Mouride "oath of loyalty"

17. Stylish in Senegal

1940, and there had been no telling when one could read of anything beyond that year. You could read in comfort in Dakar, big ceiling fans kept the air moving, and in time off you could head for the beach, excellent swimming all around the Cape Verde Peninsula.

My research wasn't always going to be that comfortable, I knew, having begun with short trips to the Region of Diourbel, a hundred or so miles inland, quite a bit hotter, and of course no beach. To set up my research, I presented it as sociology of the region, which included Touba, the Mouride capital. Those Paris contacts with the officials of the Ministry of Overseas Development proved their worth. I could drop the right names, had the right letters of introduction, most importantly to the director of a French agency, <u>Societe d'Assistance Technique et de Cooperation</u>, S.A.T.E.C., a handsome and courtly man called Pierre Chabrol. The agency's head office was in Dakar, but its French officials worked all around the interior regions, where the mission was to promote agricultural improvement, better yields especially of the main cash crop, groundnuts. My introduction took me to the director for the Region of Diourbel, and then on down the organization's hierarchy to the man in charge of the department of Mbacké, which included Touba. Those Frenchmen were doing something useful for rural Senegal, helping people to make more money, and it was more than useful for me to be locally identified as linked with their operation.

I must have been a pest, with my spiral notebooks and biro and all those questions first to French technical assistants, local civil servants and later to members of the Mouride brotherhood. I had met a rebuff or two, or what looked like the feigned absence of an informant, until I came across a young man, about my own age, a junior in S.A.T.E.C., Thierno Sow. Thierno had previously been secretary to the chief of Touba, a Senegalese government official, and he knew his way around local society. He had the deferential posture of a courtier, with a broad forehead, bright eyes and a lurking smile. He also had good French, although he hadn't gone beyond primary school. After seeing him in action around the residence of the leader of the brotherhood, I had a deal to propose to his French superiors in S.A.T.E.C. If you can detach this man from his normal duties for a time, let me work with him in and around Touba, then in return I will give a talk to the region's staff on how they might best proceed with the Mouride brotherhood's hierarchy. This was agreed with the regional director, and my research prospered.

There was a corrugated metal gate to the residence of the brotherhood's leader, the Khalifa-General, guarded by some large and portly members of the leader's entourage: to get past that gate you had to be able to say something convincing to those guards. There was never a shortage of supplicants outside, people in search of all sorts of advice or support. Some didn't get in; many had to wait a very long time. I was unusual as a white supplicant, wanting to be granted some interviews, but there was nothing automatic about my getting past that gate. I'd been held up there already, had to wait quite a while. Now, with Thierno as my guide, a discreet mutter in the ear of one of the custodians led to the gate swinging open:

we were into the court, had left the less fortunate behind. The interviews were graciously accorded. Thierno had briefed me in advance about each of the officials to be interviewed, and he introduced me to each one with the right honeyed words. First there was his introduction to the person, then the interview itself, and then the appraisal of what had been said, once the two of us were on our own.

Theirno was needed as an interpreter: my rudimentary Wolof wasn't nearly enough to work on my own. I needed him even more as a man who knew his way around court. That metal gate, the little army of hopefuls outside, the spacious, near-empty courtyard inside, gave me an image of what politics could be about, in this part of rural Africa. Another image could be added, of the disciple, prostrate or on his knees; the body language of the subject, speaking words from the time of slavery. I confess to having found all that a strange sight, and when interviewed the disciple insisted on what I would have termed his subjection. One disciple gave an account of his life of disinterested service to his holy master. When Thierno and I were alone came the comment, "He's only boasting." In and around Touba many disciples had their plans to head off to town with the blessing and support of a marabout.

Once we had seen the top people, had their approval or at least acceptance, it was possible to take our enquiries out and about in the region. Although I probably woke up more than one informant from his afternoon snooze, with Theirno's diplomacy the reception was almost always affable. I think it helped that I was asking people to talk about themselves: my reservations about their stories could be kept for our post-interview appraisal. The roof of the red Volkswagen faded to dark pink under the African sun, and I learned something about driving on sandy tracks: keep cleaning the air filter, don't try going too fast. Thierno and I became adept at changing tyres. We got to know each other pretty well as we travelled around Diourbel region.

Thierno Sow hadn't read as many books as Maurice Cowling, but he was as sceptical about professions with good intentions. He agreed with my former tutor that vanity and greed had primacy in accounting for human behaviour. When our country research was over, in April 1967, he did come down to stay with us for a time in Dakar, where we did a study of the Mouride traders and their associations. We went to the I.F.A.N. Museum, where one of the displays was of the robes worn by the leaders of anti-colonial resistance at the time of French conquest. Thierno first directed my attention to the bullet holes and all the magic writing on the robes, but leaving the museum he allowed himself a little shudder: "All the same I wouldn't want to sleep here at night." Scepticism has its limits, as in Ireland. There had been a precious moment, towards the end of our inquiries around Touba, relaxing one evening over heavily-sugared tea in the compound around his house, when he diffidently asked if he might make a personal remark. Just as diffidently, I said "Please go ahead," dreading what might be in store. Then, with a broad smile, he declared that, "To me you look just like a monkey." The red ears had given me away.

Besides Thierno Sow, another privileged informant for my study was a middle-aged Mouride cleric, Serigne Mbacké Nioro, resident in Missirah, a village some 15 miles from Touba. The title "<u>Serigne</u>" is the Wolof equivalent to the Franco-Arabic <u>Marabout</u>, commanding respect, but my friend commanded respect also as an open-minded person, with good spoken French. We had many long talks together at his home, where he explained details of belief, together with his analysis of the brotherhood's history and its organizational structure. He also wanted to know about my background, and he wanted in particular to improve his English. Rita became his tutor for several months when she joined me in the field. During our talks there was appraisal of such practices as that of the disciples' singing at religious festivals: my informant-teacher put his emphasis on the music rather than the words as far as crowd appeal was concerned. We went together to his family's place of origin at Porokhane, far to the south of Touba: my friend was from the lineage of the Mouride founder's elder brother, who had some sharp things to say about his charismatic, miracle-working junior. Serigne Mbacké Nioro was a patient teacher, gave me my view of hierarchy from the inside, and he had the look of James Joyce, spectacles and all.

The place where I was staying, a few kilometres from Touba was a government-owned house rather grandly entitled a Centre of Rural Administration (<u>Centre</u> <u>d'Encadrement</u> <u>Rural</u>). This was a modest concrete bungalow housing two junior civil servants, Alioune Kane and Saidou Ba, who very kindly agreed to put me up for the duration of my enquiries. Alioune was erect in bearing, proud of his region of origin, the Futa

Toro of Northern Senegal. Saidou was relaxed in posture, more like a student, though proud too of his region, the Casamance of southern Senegal. While different in personality, the two had quite a lot in common. For one thing neither of them was Mouride, for another they were not Wolof (the dominant ethnic community in Senegal) and then they were both young men, around my age. They had never had a white man living in their house; I had never lived in a house run by two young African men. So the three of us had a lot to learn. We talked about football. England had just won the World Cup, and Saidou was an admirer of Bobby Charlton. My hosts were a little condescending about the Mourides, among whom they worked as civil servants, and were more interested to hear about life in Ireland. They had a word or two to say about corruption in government service: one reason could be that they weren't receiving your pay.

While I loved their company, and the two of them went far out of their way to make me feel at home, there's no denying the fact that there were times when I did feel out of place. My hosts were often out in the evening, off to the local town of Mbacké on young single men's pursuits, while I stayed back to do some reading, or to write up my notes. The leisure reading was chosen to take me away from the dry savannah, books about cold or wet places, or about small-town life in the USA: Sinclair Lewis' <u>Babbitt</u> stays in mind. The horn of the local train was a consoling sound: modernity hadn't forgotten me.

A French couple living in Mbacké, Pierre and Mimi Cazaty were sometimes my hosts for an evening meal. Pierre had been with the Free French and the Royal Air Force during the war in aircraft maintenance. He came with Mimi to Senegal after the war, settling down in the little town of Mbacké where they had a busy chemist's shop and general store. His face expressed his good humour, under a French military crew-cut, and there was a wide smile from time to time. He and his wife were Catholics who had supported the political party of the Catholic Leopold Senghor from its origin in 1948. President Senghor was their friend, and Pierre served on the government's Economic and Social Council. Blonde Mimi was just as remarkable a person, the centre of local activity and good works: without her, the majorettes of Mbacké would never have been. Pierre did talk about the possibility of their retiring to France, Nice, in mind, but he went on to wonder if that would ever happen. "You know, we have a good life here, including a little place down by the sea, and there's hardly anybody left that I'm close to back home." I met Pierre in Mbacké 15 years later, by which time Mimi had died but he was still staying on, still with his rueful smile, now a defiant shrug. He reminded me of the characters in Paul Scott's Staying On.

Research students can be paranoid, anxious that the competition may be moving in on "their" space. When I came down to Dakar one Friday evening it was to hear that a multi-disciplinary team of French researchers had arrived in Dakar, to do a survey of economic, social, and political activity in the region of Diourbel, Senegal. Professor Balandier in Paris seemed to be the mastermind here. Nobody had said a word to me about this, but then I had not said much about my activities to French people either. I certainly hadn't told the Balandier that I had followed his good advice, concentrating on the Mourides. But the arrival of the French research team came at exactly the moment when my research in Touba was in full swing. So there had to be a conference: Philippe Couty and Jean Copans co-directors of the team, agreed to stay away from the Touba area until my enquiries there had come to an end (so there would be no additional researchers troubling my informants), and I agreed to let them know what I had found, once it was written up. The French team's findings, when they were written up, proved to be more than helpful to me. There was detailed work on labour time, landholdings, making the essential point that those extravagantly deferential disciples put their own economic interests first. The holy men got what was left over, in labour time and money: the abject-looking disciples had a careful eye on what was good for themselves.

Dakar and the Completion of Fieldwork

I was at one with them there, looking after myself: the austerity of my living arrangements in Ndame, the miles and miles of sandy tracks, the notebooks and the biro, all that was from Monday morning to Friday afternoon. About four o'clock on Friday it was back into the little car and off towards Dakar: there is a point on that journey when the road starts to zigzag down from the plateau toward the Cape Verde peninsula. The temperature begins to drop as you near the ocean, you may pick up a little breeze, and in my case you knew you were getting near to town and to Rita. There would be another social world, people from the University and the research institutes, local friends as well as friends from France or the USA There would be a lot of the beach with a frisbee or wiffleball, beer and good food. Progressive-type French people didn't really approve of my time spent with enemies of socialism in Touba and Americans thought it must be tough living in such primitive conditions. This latter point gave me a chance to make a fool of myself.

There was a dinner party given by Fred Hayward, an American political scientist and his wife Lori: eight people at table. Talk turned to how hard it must be for me to have to do without the things we take for granted in the city. "Oh," said I. "things aren't so bad. There is a Lebanese cinema in Mbacké, a schoolteacher to talk to, lots of local action. It's about as good as Sioux Falls, South Dakota." Lori Hayward went beetroot red: "Bob is from Sioux Falls." Robert H. Legvold, across the table from me, was a political scientist doing a thesis on Soviet influence in Africa. He said that he didn't take offence at my remark, but did leave me wondering what on earth had made me pick his town out of the hat. I had never been there; it had crossed my consciousness a few days before in a New Yorker cartoon.

The road back to Ndame and Touba started at 6 a.m. on Monday: I got up early to avoid the heat of the day and the traffic on the road. I also wished to leave enough time to organize the day's interviews. There was release in store for the patient Mourides, the time would come when that notebook would be closed up and the inquisitive young white man would point his way back towards Dakar, one last time.

That was the day when I discovered that mice had been taking straw from my mattress to build a nest for themselves in the corner of the bedroom. Sometimes at night I had heard scratching sounds, but that hadn't troubled my sleep. My hosts roared laughing, before they bade me an affectionate farewell. Alioune gave me a Tukulor ceremonial dagger in a coloured leather holster, saying "You taught us something." I bashfully said that I didn't know that much. He then said, "That's not what I mean". So I suppose that for my hosts I had been something new in the way of white men. The two of them had certainly been something new for me. As I drove back to Dakar that last time, I sang to myself the Nat King Cole song, "The Party's Over."

Travels in Casamance

Saidou Ba had long been saying how much he would like to take us to see some of his own region of Casamance, south of the Gambia. We took him up on that offer, as the three of us went to Sedhiou, his hometown, staying in his family's house. Along the way we crossed the River Gambia, part of an ex-British colony, now a small independent state, 20 miles wide, and 200 miles long. In the Casamance one evening we travellers came across four elderly men, half-naked in the oppressive heat, around a Monopoly set laid out on a raffia mat: "Old Kent Road," "Park Lane", without their having any English between them. This reminded me of a previous moment, much nearer to Touba, when I had come across an old man asleep on a mat on the edge of a field, his transistor radio still on. "Dexter plays forward," those were the first words to reach me: it was bizarre. He was obviously listening to the BBC Overseas Service, as it was then called.

Saidou Ba had already briefed me on some of the attitudes to expect in his native region, where people talked of "going to Senegal" when they went north across the Gambia. They knew very well, he said, that Casamance too is a region of Senegal and only a few in the region were really separatists, but it was remarkable enough to the newcomer that the place looked and felt rather different from the rest of the country. Towards the sea, in lower Casamance is a tropical rainforest, a great contrast to the semi-desert terrain further north. Catholic missionaries had been active, especially in lower Casamance, and the French language was more widely understood. We pioneer tourists went to a very beautiful beach, at Bukut Ouolof, not far from where the Club Mediterranée would later set up a resort. Rita and I went swimming while Saidou stayed at the edge of the beach, smiling broadly, altogether dignified in his long white kaftan.

Leaving Senegal and Completing our Degrees in London

When Rita and I went back to Dakar, Saidou went back to work in Ndame: we O'Brien's were back to work too, in the capital city. With Thierno Sow I went to see some of the Mouride associations' leaders in Dakar. There was a good deal of derisive laughter, as the leaders of different associations questioned each other's claims on membership numbers. But there wasn't much question, overall, that these people were doing well in street trade, building from the bottom up: cheap sunglasses, a single aspirin for your headache. These people would go on to prosper, with trading networks in Europe and the USA, networks of commercial trade held together by religious trust. In New York City Mayor Koch welcomed them as being like the Jews of the City's previous times.

Rita kept me up to date with news of her research among the French, who were as hospitable to her as were the Mourides to me. Whether with business people or technical assistants, she told me that she did encounter a prevalent scepticism regarding Senegalese working patterns and practices. There was a moment, in our little house, when I had forgotten or neglected to attend to some domestic matter. Collapsing on the bed, convulsed in helpless giggles, she pointed an accusing finger up to me with the repeated words, "<u>manque de conscience professionelle</u>". So I too was part of the new Africa.

The Cape Verde peninsula has its own micro-climate, for two-thirds of the year there are the cooling Atlantic breezes, any excuse was good to be off to the beach. Rita and I were at the same time increasingly attentive to the hoarding of our field-notes. They all went into a metal trunk for transfer back on the <u>Ancerville</u> at the end of our stay, together with our other belongings, the Mouride paintings on glass my particular treasure. I sat on that case of field-notes to ensure there'd be no casual thieving while we were in port in Las Palmas (Canary Islands), on the way back to Marseille.

We were a single-minded pair that next year, writing up those notes in London, getting our Ph.D. theses ready for examination in 1969. Rita's oral exam came when she was heavily pregnant. Mr. Woolf, still the man in charge, had given his order that she should at all times have her feet up. The examiners caused her no trouble. Neither did my oral examiners, a little earlier in the year, so we each of us had our doctorates, those precious blue-bound volumes.

Much more important, our baby daughter, Sarah Estelle, was born in Hackney Hospital. I saw her before Rita, who had had a caesarean section and was recovering from the anaesthetic. My words to Tony Woolf, as we looked down at that tiny, perfect shape on a hospital sheet, were to the effect that this was as much his achievement as it was mine. To which he responded, "My own feeling exactly." I bought a small packet of Hamlet cigars at the pub along the road, didn't share them with anyone. The sun shone through the dirty window. I had just come from seeing the beautiful beginning of a new world for us in Hackney Hospital, London E9.

CHAPTER 8

Refining Ambition: London, Dakar, Algiers

The Start of a Career

"How is Donal?" That was the question put to Rita by Professor Ernest Gellner at the end of a long lunch in the LSE dining room in 1966. "Oh, Donal's fine: just worried about getting a job." Rita told me about this on the way home with the news that Gellner had reassured her as to my future employment. He said he knew a man called Vox Populus (and here Rita got the giggles) at the School of Oriental and African Studies, a place that is expanding with a go-ahead Director, (Sir) Cyril Phillips. Gellner's friend, Professor P.J. Vatikiotis did then ring up, inviting me to join him for lunch at a Greek restaurant in Charlotte Street. I had a mousakka though the professor warned me off the retsina (filthy stuff) so I had a glass or two of the Greek white wine and we got stuck into the way Americans teach political science. "Scientists!" - A laugh or two at the expense of Gabriel Almond or Talcott Parsons. Vatikiotis looked on politics as a seedy business about which Greeks had a say long ago. He had worked in the USA, could drop the names of some of the important figures; many American political scientists were his personal friends, including Morris Janowitz of the University of Chicago.

Vatik wanted to impress me, and in his way succeeded. More important was for me to impress him. Ernest Gellner had prepared my ground having given a puff for my still incomplete thesis in sociology. Political sociology, not so far away from what Americans call political science, so there was no fuss on that score. The first degree in history tended to weigh in my favour as much perhaps as my two years at the University of California. It certainly seemed to help that I didn't seem to have been blinded by American science, while also knowing some of the right American names to drop, with a plausible manner of giving them mention; a little perhaps like a courtship. One American name in particular, that of Fred Riggs, a political scientist specializing in the study of Thailand, he seemed to make the right impression. I could see that Vatikiotis took his distance from the view that Asia or Africa would ever develop in the direction of democratic modernity, the view then at least nominally espoused by the leading figures in the study of international comparative politics. Gabriel Almond, in the lead. Riggs theory was that Asia, not Africa, was developing not into democracy but into a sorry mess of corruption and dictatorship not far from gangster politics. My case to Vatikioitis was that Riggs writings on Asia were if anything even more relevant to Africa which he hadn't studied at all. Riggs "theory of prismatic society" had been written in a tortured vocabulary, defying the reader: not many people in the United States had chosen to take up that terminology challenge. Vatikiotis had made a try, but it looked to me as if he had given up early. He was however apparently, willing to give me some credit for doing unusual reading.

One name that I didn't need to drop was during the Greek lunch was my famous father. As I was often enough to find, Conor worked more effectively in my favour when he was unmentioned. Professor Vatikiotis did at last, casually enough, mention of a post that he had in mind, very junior in African politics. I said that this would be an excellent idea and thanked him for the lunch. I also said how much I enjoyed the conversation.

So I had my reasons to hope as I walked away from Charlotte Street. Then, for more than a week, nothing – not a word from Professor Vatikiotis. Egged on, no doubt by Rita, I picked up the phone to the professor in SOAS asking very tentatively if any steps were being taken for the interviews for the kind of junior post that he had mentioned over lunch. "No," came the answer, "You've been interviewed." You got the job. Then he asked me to come into the Department of Economic and Political Studies for a meeting to discuss what I would be expected to do. The head of department was an American economist, Edith Penrose who said that she wanted to be sure to have me on the department's books even though I'd be away in Senegal doing the PhD field research 1966-1967. I wouldn't be paid while away but would be entitled to that year as part of part of my pensionable service. The offer of an extra year's pension was a long way from my immediate concern, but it's nice to be wanted even a little bit and it was flattering that she sought to prevent me from going off to another university. I signed the relevant form and we beamed at each other. I'd be teaching African studies from the autumn of 1967. Those were times of recruitment on a grand scale at SOAS, remembered by a later Director as the year when we were sweeping them in off the streets; not far off for the junior lectureship in African politics in 1967.

Teaching duties at SOAS in African studies turned out to be a very long way short of onerous, one two term class on African states, every week in term time, and a light teaching load that suited me very well, while working my doctoral research. Colleagues in the department were from, all over the place: Egypt, the United States, Germany, Iraq …and Ireland. A Department head a few years later, mentioned that this was getting to be like Cairo airport - as good a place as any for an Irish immigrant.

Among the colleagues, were the restless souls of the SOAS Left Group to which I was briefly affiliated. My impertinent pamphlet "What is Wrong with SOAS?" was written for the Group's internal discussions and circulated around the school, without consulting the author. (I tried to destroy every copy I could find) Serves him right, you may say, and I would not contest the point. At the time, on the threshold of my interview for a tenure appointment, I did feel betrayed by the leftists, which made me begin to think about my place on the left. This was a time of student politics. Paris in May 1968, a place of time and reference. But then I hadn't even been comfortable with the shroud of self-righteousness of Berkeley, four years earlier, with the Yankee <u>soixant huitards</u>. Did the future belong to us? Was I part of us?

There were good reasons for doubt on either of these questions, either that the students were going to make a world so very different or that I felt comfortable with their idealism. Twenty seven years old by 1968, I was very much aware of the need to make a living, the kind of person the Berkeley students would have called "a fink." Why would a fink write a pamphlet mocking the people he hoped would be his employers? It's only a partial answer to say that the author never expected it to go public in the school. Striking a posture among the troublemakers? A backhanded way of saying farewell to the Left? Those are the questions I put to myself now, at the time it felt like the temptation of impudence. If anything, it was mocking my colleagues on the Left. Forget that SOAS was subservient to capitalism and imperialism: the place is boring!

One gorgeously dressed research student, member of our group, Fred Halliday, had extended his sympathy in my direction at this time. Fred was of Irish origin, Ampleforth-educated a very convincing drawl to go with his beige jacket and beautiful long hair. He was on the Editorial Board of the New Left Review, as fashionable as you can get. He helped me indirectly by tormenting P.J. Vatikiotis in his course on Comparative Politics. Vatik expressed his exasperation to me on this score, and in effect passed me the course. So I was now at the centre at the Department, thanks to Fred and his new left condescension. Not that Fred was particularly impressed by the way that I taught Comparative Politics, starting from Weber, Marx and the Italian Elitists (Pareto and Mosca): theoretical pluralism? A raised eyebrow but I did also get a hint of a gentle complicit smile, and not a word about Ireland.

New Departures

A lot of things happened in 1969, a turning point as far as the O'Brien family was concerned. Rita and I both got doctorates that year when our daughter Sarah Estelle was born. And that was just for openings. In the same year, my career was lined up in SOAS, to be my employer for 39 years.

1969 was also the year the provisional IRA set off on its campaign of bombing, shooting and physical intimidation. In the same year, my father took the decision to return to Ireland responding to an invitation from Ireland's Labour Party to stand as a deputy in the Dail Eireann. For Conor to do this, he had to leave a very well appointed university post at NYU. He was often to London in this period, and we saw more of him. His son Patrick was adopted in the same year.

In the meanwhile, there were decisions to be made about our own residence in London or in the country. Rita had a fellowship at the Institute of Development Studies, Sussex, Donal his teaching at the School of Oriental and African Studies, London. Where were we to live with tiny Sarah?

The first option was Sussex, thanks to some important people who crossed our paths in London. Joanna Drew of the Arts

Council mentioned at a party that she had a friend who might be able to help out. So off I went to Sussex to see (Sir) Roland Penrose and the house he had in mind eventually for his son Tony. Burgh Hill House was an elegant Georgian structure, three stories, lots of ground upon which was a Spanish chestnut tree and notably, a Picasso ceramic tile set over the Aga. Lots of rooms recently decorated. I did thank Sir Roland for showing it all but said that it was far beyond our means. The reply was a question: "How much do you pay for your flat in London?" "Twelve pounds a week was my reply" "That'll be fine," he said. So with a broad smile, the deal was done. Looking back on that, I suppose this was negotiation. The O'Brien assets were those of the very young, perhaps as University people, we would be moving on, getting out in time for Tony Penrose to move in. Maybe Conor was a little help too - a good calling card. Conor was respectable, frequently a columnist in The Observer, read by people of liberal political views in those days.

Roland Penrose was a man of great charm and traditional country dress with a broad smile. He and his wife, the photographer Lee Miller were regularly our hosts at Farley Farm together with us some important people from the world of art. Paintings by Picasso, Max Ernst, Joan Miró filled the ground floor rooms. The Penrose's were the most considerate of hosts, as the landlord role blurred into the background. Roland perhaps wanted to educate us in country ways, with humour and charm as well as generosity. Taking fashion photographs for Vogue, Lee had worked with Man Ray and as a war photographer with the American army in Germany. In

Berlin, her reply to all that was a remarkable photograph of herself in Hitler's bathtub. Life in rural Sussex must have been a bit down on such a career but Lee did take a mild interest in the new tenants that Roland had found for Burgh Hill House. We tenants founds ourselves placed comfortably enough in the local social hierarchy and often invited to dinner at the weekends by the squire, which left me feeling more than unusually a fraud. The feeling was altogether different in this period when I would go up to London for two days a week, staying with Abbas and Madge Keledar. The train journey from Lewes to London took me to the blessed anonymity of the big city. Arriving at Victoria Station the first in breath of big city air: "Ah, bliss - there nobody knew who you were or cared.

The Onset of MS

Another thing happened in 1969: I started to limp walking across Lambeth Bridge on one of the long walks I took, as Rita was keeping her feet up at home while she was pregnant. Here was just a little shuffle, an inconvenience, but also a puzzle. At about this same time, there were some symptoms, an eye affliction, a dropped jam jar, in each case on my right side, the same side as the limp. The fact that I noted each of these occurrences on the same side of my body shows that I expected some coincidences here. On the other hand, however, I desperately didn't want to know, clinging to the idea, that I was just being a hypochondriac, a 'malade imaginaire'.

Was I being a hypochondriac about these strange medical symptoms? It would have been nice if that were so: I'd be part of the crowd. There was a conversation with German guests, Hermann and Isobel Schroder at Burgh Hill House (1970) – a moment of conviviality when we agreed that all three of us are hypochondriacs, and a laughing matter. But then Hermann mused, "What if he is really ill?" That was a question which hung heavily in the air. At one level, I was all too aware of the reality of my symptoms, the bouts of blurred vision in one eye or another, of acute pain in the eye and also of double vision, all coming at intervals of three to six months from 1969 onwards. The doctors told me it was optic neuritis, and prescribed a course of steroid injections or pills but the symptoms returned as they had before, in a slightly diminished form. I suppose I knew they were not telling the whole story; how could an eye problem make you limp? But I never put the simple question to the people who could have given me an answer.

The period 1969 to 1974 was the worst of it (so far). Rita had a cry at the beginning, the two of us in Sarah's little bedroom with the orange wallpaper in Kennington Road. I tried to comfort her then, but inside I was just as dismayed. The symptoms of the next few years made me turn in on myself. There were several short stays in hospital, time for darker thoughts. If things were to go on like this, bouts of inflammation frequently, maybe I'm not going to live that long? And if so, maybe that would be just as well, as I would be less of a burden on Rita and Sarah. That was the darkest moment, alone. Rita felt that it was time I was trying to sort things out, by becoming less self-absorbed. I didn't know what to do, even what to think; certainly did not want to be seen with a walking stick.

Now I know this isn't fair to the player, Kevin Hector, of the splendid team of the time, Derby County, but the memory of watching them in St. Pancras Hospital stands out as one of the bleakest moments. What's the point? What did I know or care? But perhaps that moment was one of turning around, a dawn of self-realisation as I turned the telly off. OK, you're ill. What are you going to do about it? Not long after this, at an outpatient appointment at University College Hospital in 1971 by accident, I overheard the name of my illness, muttered over the shoulder to a group of students, Multiple Sclerosis. Dr Robin Vickery seemed to be surprised that I asked for a confirmation of what I had overheard. "Didn't you know?" And then very gently, he spelled out the rules: the most common of neurological illnesses, not fatal, a very wide range of possible symptoms which might or might not be severe. I wasn't to look it up in a medical reference book: "You'll only imagine yourself in a worse situation; for lots of people the symptoms never occur. I was to deal with the symptoms as they came; they were treatable and I should get on with my life. There was a normal life expectancy. There is a great deal that you can do for yourself, starting with physiotherapy.

Coming to Terms with MS

Was I relieved to know? Perhaps so, at some level, but I soon learned that it wasn't news to pass generally about, and watch the faces fall. Rita learned first and took it on as a challenge to both of us: we'd deal with it. Lady Greene already knew it was my illness, as she had consulted Jonathan Miller, a friend - a neurologist and author. Elaine supposed I'd never ask. She had been a close advisor to me, many Turkish meals near her literary agency in Newington Green, but we'd skirted around the subject until then. Dr. William Goody gave excellent advice, but also kept clear of the name. All the doctors knew I was a straight-forward case of relapsing- remitting MS. But the patient did not want to know, and the doctors held their tongues. The collusion of doctor and patient had been one. I had never asked.

One doctor in the early stages of my illness did warn me against the danger of ambition: "Treat your symptoms as a witch warning." I took the advice into consideration, and my small ambitions were fulfilled in initially at the School. A psychiatrist gave me a warning of another kind when I asked her about the dangers of an emotional kind – given my illness. I mentioned my father and with a smirk, and said that perhaps I was trying to compete with him. She answered straight-faced that she did not know my father, hadn't met him, but from what she knew about him she felt it might be better to identify rather than compete. I mentioned the conversation to John Silverlight of The Observer who roared with laughter and clapped me on the back and said, "Wasn't that obvious?"

When I told my father I had MS in 1971 he subsequently wrote the following:

Never having experienced the challenge of anything like the magnitude of that which you (and Rita with you) have been facing and are facing, there is little that I can say that will be of any help. You know how I feel, I think, and you and I are both a bit dumb about expressing such feelings. Just one thing, though, I know a bit about you, not everything, but something, I think you are supremely well equipped to meet severe stress. You can gauge its severity justly, without exaggeration, evasion or panic. It's true that you are both exceptionally sensitive and exceptionally imaginative, so that you must have suffered even more acutely than most people would under the initial impact of this thing. But you also have unusually deep inner resources, moral, emotional, and intellectual, great powers of recuperation, reflection and enjoyment, and also the mysterious, indestructible and versatile capacity that we vaguely call humour. You see I have learned a bit about you since I scolded you for breaking your leg. It's true that we have both been through a bit, both together, separately, and not quite together, not quite separately, since my previous appearance as a Spartan therapist.

After Conor, Christine had nothing as eloquent or comforting to say: her face expressed simple panic when I told her about the diagnosis in a restaurant in London. She took Rita aside on that occasion and asked for a prognosis, which was, of course, an impossibility. I know that there were occasions when Christine could show pure steel and an engaging gaiety, but family illnesses were never her strong point. In a way there was a collusion between two very shy people tip-toeing around something they knew she never wished to address. I didn't really miss the warmth and support which might have come from my mother, though I never doubted that she loved me. By that time, I had already found surrogate mothers in Elaine Greene and Cecilia Gillie – two people who never shied from expressing warmth and empathy, as well as proffering excellent life lessons.

Maurice Kogan, an Islington neighbour and friend, put it another way a few years later, "Donal, you have a beautiful wife and a beautiful daughter. What's your problem?" Sarah was a great help encouraging me back into the world. She urged me to take her to the sweet shop in the Essex Road and get over my reluctance to get out at all and be seen with my walking stick. It was about the time I was coming out of my reclusive phase, which lasted about five years. Rita sometimes later referred to it as my "Job period." I have always thought that I valued the indifference of other people and shared that thought with my friend Will Plowden (who sadly died of cancer in 2010). Will asked, "What happens if you need other people?" asked almost as a moral question and a good question for someone with MS. Stated rather gently, as he did, I had to agree with him. I think what I meant by indifference was the search for privacy in my condition, not wishing people to find me pitiable.

Once on a holiday in the West of Ireland, Sarah, Rita and I were in Galway High Street buying extra rain gear, preparing for a flight to Inisheer in the Aran Islands. I was outside the shop in my wheelchair and an old women came along and thrust 2s 6d into my hand. I was totally shocked and tried to return it yet she said, it might have been something I have done to you."

MS teaches you that self-pity is the great enemy, or making "the poor mouth," as it would be in Ireland. This is something which came to mind when going together with a group of "sufferers" to use a Hyperbaric Oxygen tank - which was recommended as something of a fad in the 1970s for MS patients. I don't know how much good the oxygen did, but I do know that breathing in self-pity was a useful learning experience from this perspective. Against all that was the simple value of doing your exercises. The remnants of an incompetent rugby player, eventually using a standing frame, a walking frame - all of that. It helped to keep me in reasonable shape, as well as maintaining my self-respect. Someone with MS can forget about private medical insurance, but you can totally rely on NHS medical provision, in my experience. They tell you often that a great deal is down to you and your attitude.

House prices in London were going up steeply in the early 1970s when we had settled into rural Sussex. If they continued much longer, the O'Brien's would not be able to move there. In the long run London was the place most likely to accommodate two separate careers. You can perhaps hear the voices of special pleading here, my case as put to Rita. We looked for several months in affordable locations and finally bought a home in Islington from a West Indian, Joe Padilla, who wanted to go back to Barbados for the sake of his wife and children. He came back to see us years later. He was very pleased with the results of the sale for all the family. The Padillas of Ockendon Road had managed by letting many rooms to West Indian tenants who filled the narrow four storied house. A lot had to be changed from the greasy cooking in many of the rooms. We three O'Brien's were displacing many West Indians but the trouble was with the Padillas, not ourselves. We were just the buyers in a busy house market, purchasing with the financial assistance of Elaine Greene (who had seen us through some appalling times in 1960 when he returned from the Congo). She was now godmother to Sarah and in truth to all of us. She had come down to stay many weekends in Burgh Hill usually bearing generous gifts and passed her country knowledge on to us, new recruits. I had become quite a keen vegetable gardener at Burgh Hill, even went as far as entering for the largest potato competition at the village fair. Elaine took one look at my hoped-for potato entry, snorted and told me that I did not have a chance of winning the competition, as there had been much bigger potato entries she had customarily seen in village fairs in Suffolk. Intimidated, I backed down and did not enter the competition. But we all went along to the fair and the winning potato was smaller than my combatant. Elaine consoled us with the case of champagne, but she knew that I would have passed up all the fizz for that coveted local recognition.

There was no denying the beauties of the Sussex countryside, from the bluebell wood near the farmhouse to the Downland and the coast for long walks and outings. We got to know a bit about wild flowers and identified bee orchids. But Elaine could see that our sights were in the city and offered to help in many ways. Buying a house in London with a two year old daughter born there, this Irish immigrant was committed to a long-term future in the United Kingdom. This is where we wanted to be. Rita and I each had our teaching incomes, supplemented by taking in a lodger and a foreign au pair for help looking after Sarah. As she grew, she went to play group at the local infants' school and formed friendships with local children, as well as those of Indian neighbours. She was soon more of a Londoner than either of her parents with a plausible London glottal stop. She did come to Ireland for family visits, liked Howth and the scenery, but was always glad to get back to Islington. On one occasion on our return from Dublin, we brought with us a bottle of Irish whiskey for our Irish next door neighbours, Matty and Mary Fahey. Mary was a bus conductor, a very amiable person, looked at the label and raised an eyebrow which broke into an amiable smile, with the following verdict, "Ah sure, you could not afford Scotch!"

Advice to Conor: "Staying Alive in Ireland"

In 1971, my father became Minister of Communications in the Dublin government, was prompt and eloquent in his denunciation, not only of the Provos, but most especially of the respectable people in the Republic in their concealed complicity. This made me think about my father's exposed position, the house well away from neighbours or observers. It did take two years to come to the decision to write to him with what I hoped might be some helpful advice in the practicality of self-preservation. Bernard Levin in a column at the time had praised my father as the sanest man in Ireland. Levin's verdict prompted me to write the following to Conor on 20 September 1971. Conor had certainly been brave and lucid on the subject of the Provisional IRA and its fellow travellers, call it saintly or call it courage, either way, he was close to isolation.

How to Stay Alive in Ireland
A personal and Political Programme for my Father

a) Your sincere cooperation in this enterprise is expected, knowing you, I don't really think that you are likely to follow all the suggestions set out below. But please do try to adhere to the advice in the general way in which it is intended.

b) There will be times when discretion is particularly important; when your enemies feel themselves to be on the defensive, be very careful. When they find themselves to be defeated, like now.

c) There are, as you have mentioned, some things (people, ideas) that are more important to you than your own life. You must work out very carefully what these are and try to minimise them as far as possible especially the ideas. I cannot recommend wholesale sacrifice of family members.

Recommended:
1. All the more discreet aspects of political activity, which may also be those where close reasoning, persuasion, (the

things you are good at) may have some possible effect. Lobbying, personal communication with influentials, letters to same, not for publication, unpublicised apparatchik activity and so forth.

2. Travel as often as possible, as far outside Ireland as possible. Any pretext would be good. This will not only help to remove you as a physical target but also prevent you from developing dangerous parochial obsessions.

3. Hire (or buy) a properly trained dog. Whatever the truth of your recent domestic incident (a prowler, or attempted break-in). This really is important in determining vagrant malevolent parties or violent lunatics.

4. Write think pieces, preferably long with abstract and complex arguments. Be short on named names for publication which is unlikely to have wide readership among wild lunatics.

5. Cultivate studied inconspicuousness. Suppress the marked glint in your eye, also suppress spontaneous movement of facial muscles (these can often be far too revealing at the personal level).

Discouraged:
1. Talk or write in public with excessive frequency on issues regarded as important by violent lunatics. As far as possible, find people who share similar views. This is not only for your safety; it is also politically effective.

2. Be too conspicuous by your "sanity" or any other qualities publically attributed to you. These qualities notably include intelligence and lucidity. All efforts to disguise or at least mute the public exercise of some of these qualities. Adopting certain qualities alien to you may be an occasional help. I can think of circumstances when it might be expedient to have a mask of temporary madness and merge into the background.

3. Make any public criticism of named violent lunatics or their friends. Keep it on a general level.

4. Appear in public (or indeed in private) places known to be frequented by violent lunatics. In general, the less you appear in public the better. This includes TV.

5. Write open letters to anybody.

6. Be provocative. You have a dangerous gift in this direction. Verbal barbs as you well know may be returned with quite other weaponry.

7. Become a national psychotherapist. And if it does look as if you are the last sane man left, get the hell out of Ireland.

Footnote: There are, I am aware, alternative strategies but there is one I strongly dis-recommend – maximizing your public appearance in the national cause. Engaging in public debate with IRA men was particularly un-recommended. The more points you score, the more tempted they will be to reply in their own language. This would suggest that your safety would be conspicuous, making it publicly too costly for your enemies to do you in. I believe that such a strategy might be valid in other circumstances, but not in yours. The enemy is too ill-disciplined and prone to national failings (booze, insanity). For them to calculate along these lines, note that cost benefit analysis is not the strength of the national movement.

With love in the hope that some of this may be helpful,
Donal

Conor's reply from Dail Eireann on 28th September was to thank me for the letter; "and the very good advice it contains. All the recommendations I can accept. As regards 3, I have bought for a small sum a rather large dog. To call him properly trained would be an exaggeration, but I think he is all right for the purpose. As regards 5, I am doing my best with this one and also trying to bring some equivalent of it into my prose style. I have been very impressed with the reply of the Anglican Divine Hooker to a cantankerous puritanical opponent; 'the more points you score, the more tempted they will be to reply in their own language'. "Your letter," Hooker wrote, "consists in equal parts of raillery and of reason. To your raillery, I make no reply, to your reason, I reply as follows – it is difficult to live up to but I shall do my best". As regards the "Discouraged" points, most of this I can take my debate with the IRA man which is to take place, but he belongs to the official group (Sinn Féin).

Looking back on my letter now, I am not sure how much it did help my father. I used the term violent lunatics too many times and borrowing unconsciously perhaps from Bernard Levin. In the footnote, I may have got it plain wrong. Conor did go for the alternative strategy of conspicuousness, often on TV and it may be that this was his preservation. He did learn from where I know not, that the Ruling Council of the Provisional IRA decided against killing him on the grounds that it would be counter - productive. If that were so, I had underestimated the cost benefit analysis made by the national movement and also the discipline. There was cold logic behind what I called insanity, but I was right to warn him against naming names.

SOAS: the Institution as Hero

SOAS supported me though these years. Nothing was ever mentioned, but they were well aware of the situation. They supplied the facilities and the special latitude to have a doze after lunch in my office, thus missing out on the most boring meetings of the School's governance. I never asked for these – they were given. At times when the ups and downs of MS meant that I could not make it to the School, I would call the Department secretary who would organize taxis and the students came to Islington where I taught the class in my dressing gown in the bedroom. Later, when I had to use a wheelchair, the School installed ramps and rails. As a consequence, I came to have a well-grounded materially based loyalty to the institution. They saw me through the full age of retirement at the age of 65, for many years prior to that as a full professor in my department – all of that and MS as well.

The collegiality and good friendships especially with the porters and lower level staff who helped me in and out of the building was very important. The porters sometimes had to be called if I fell in my office. Professor Oliver commented that my disability must be useful for finding parking spaces. Otherwise no one much mentioned my illness. And the silence suited me well. I never gave up the desire for promotion, but it rather slid into the background in comparison to life with MS.

My naughty text on the School being boring with reference to "oriental despotism" as its mode of governance, bringing in the Director of the School and Professor Bernard Lewis (an authority on Turkey and the Middle East). These people did not react to my text or even mention it. They made no effort to impede my progress up the academic ladder from lecturer to professor.

As the illness unfolded, so my career developed. At a tenure interview in 1972, the Director asked me if I had anything new to add to the documentation already available. I told him that my PhD thesis had been accepted by the Clarendon Press. With a smile, the Director said, "That's nice, but would you please share with the Committee your thoughts on student discipline." I waffled about a staff-student committee, the kind of thing we had been discussing in the SOAS Left Group. Professor Oliver asked a double question: "Wouldn't that be time-consuming? Would it be a good use of your time?" When I left the room, the Secretary of the School, Mr. Bracken, I was later told by Professor Oliver said, "I would not touch that young man with a barge pole." And Sir Cyril, it was reported answered, "Don't be silly!" He had seen through my showing off, I've no doubt. So, bravo to SOAS for taking me on. Repressive tolerance? Not that much to repress, Phillips and Oliver could see. Father – son? Ambitious twerp?

The teaching structure of the School at post-graduate level was organized around the teaching of degrees – MA in African Studies, MSc in Political Studies. That brought me into regular contact with fellow Africanists and students of politics. How could you be bored? There were always people to talk to, and learn from. Prof Oliver's History seminar was a wonderful piece of showmanship – those eyebrows – the terror of students and department colleagues alike. As a political scientist, though, I was a free man. What Roland Oliver was doing – apart from his reign of terror, was making African Studies respectable for historians; those letters from him with the return address from The Athenaeum. Berkeley had been making African Studies respectable. Oral tradition was in the vanguard of this kind of research – archaeology, too, while the reality was mostly the study of colonial archives. Richard Rathbone of the History Department was a very key link man. I also attended the anthropology seminars at University College, where Murray Las was another key man.

As for Political Studies, the Department (at the time I joined it - Economic and Political Studies) there was almost an immediate crisis. The students had been making so many complaints about the teaching of comparative politics by Professor Vatikiotis that he was anxious to unload it. I stepped up to the mark and said I would be delighted, which was almost true. My contribution to the teaching of comparative politics or political sociology was to bring in the work of Barrington Moore (The Social Origins of Dictatorship and Democracy: Lord and Peasant in the Modern World). That was something which clearly marked a difference from the way the course had been previously taught. The students did not try to walk out or throw orange peels at the teacher, so I suppose I was doing my bit to create intellectual order. Looking around at the students or at the members of staff, I was impressed by how many were not-in-the-full-Irish-sense Brits. Ruth McVey from the US, Abbas Keledar from Iraq, not to speak of Prof. Vatik himself from Alexandria, Stuart Schramm from the US. Add it all up: for an Irishman it was a kind of home.

In the Staff Common Room, one saw the ascendancy of Professor Lewis, a man with a particularly elegant sneer, deployed ferociously around the room at one party or another. There was one historian of Africa, in particular, Douglas Jones, who usually earned the most withering of all Prof. Lewis' smirks and sneers, directed in fact at all of the history of Africa and the teaching of it.

Our Department office was a much cosier and more welcoming place, probably because it was run by the Department Secretary, the surrogate mother of this multi-cultural family. Colleagues made allowances for other's weaknesses; department meetings were occasions for trading off teaching responsibilities. Looking back on what seemed like an enthusiastic selfless gesture by my offer to take over

Comparative Politics, it certainly was a bid for a more secure place for myself in the Department. It was a core course for all students doing the MSc.

Irishness scarcely came into Department life. Conor was my silent partner; nobody was quite impertinent enough to ask for his telephone number or anything of the sort. He did come in to collect me on one occasion and Vatik tried patronizing him. I could almost hear my father biting his lip and saying nothing whatever. Other remarkable features of that Department included Professor Schramm, who used to hurl furniture around his office. He also talked to his filing cabinet. What he appeared to be doing was to try to impress the rest of us that he was a man of the world.

From 1969 to 1972, I was Editor of the Journal of Development Studies, which I regarded as a good career move. But it was not without its fraught moments with my fellow Directors. An American economist, Wolfgang Stolper sent in an article which was reviewed most unfavourably by a young Michael Lipton, a brilliant but outspoken Oxford economist. I had no idea who Stolper was or that the article had been recruited by the distinguished Professor Paul Streeten of the Editorial Board, specifically to enhance the reputation of this fledgling academic journal which had as yet little standing among economists. The whole incident – in which I got caught unwittingly in the middle was, I remember very stressful. My days at the JDS were greatly lightened, though, by a young Jim Muir, the publisher's editorial man. Jim, who is one of the most distinguished commentators on the Middle

East, working for the BBC and currently based in Beruit was in those days a recent Cambridge graduate with a first in Arabic. Jim had a wonderful sense of humour, which really kept me afloat during fraught moments with senior academic colleagues. We were discussing a particularly boring article by a Dutch academic, whom I described as "no high flyer." Jim provided me with a cartoon captioned "Beware of low flying authors," which was pinned to the side of my filing cabinet for decades.

I was pleased to be able to complete <u>Saints and Politicians</u>, my second book and get it successfully published. I tried to make it a bolder more striking version of my original research, making it hopefully more accessible to a general audience, assisted by the wonderful cover photo of the head of the brotherhood clothed in white sharing an intimate thought with President Senghor. <u>The Mourides of Senegal,</u> the essential scholarly text of my original research. It got an excellent review from John Dunn of Kings, Cambridge in <u>The Spectator</u> who described it as "poised, direct, humane and disturbing...." When <u>Saints and Politicians</u> was published, John wrote further praise in a personal letter. He described it as "a proper book about Africa for the first time and since I have not been invited to say so in public, I wanted you to know that I thought it <u>excellent</u>. It is simply in a different <u>class</u> than all those books about Africa which clutter our shelves. It's the adult voice which I miss so much normally. I read books about Africa with patient condescension (and I am seldom disappointed in my expectation). I think it's a model, <u>S&P</u>, much better than the first book, clear, economical, stylish, very funny and in the end, as the message sinks home, very powerful. I hope people notice how special it is, in proper public places." Rita had told me as much (in tears) when she read the final manuscript, and this letter from John was a great boost.

Being Irish could be a teaching asset, certainly so with African students, but also more generally. I tried disengaging myself from the patronising tone of most of the literature. When it came to ethnicity, or call it tribalism, Northern Ireland was leading the way in those days. One could also say that the Irish led the way in the wars of national liberation in the twentieth century. We were the first: rural flying columns, the importance of propaganda and deception. And since the leaders of the anti-colonial armies devoured the literature of all previous actors in the same situation, Ireland played a hugely important role.

The tribal situation can be in one's bloodstream: "It was the biggest mix-up you have ever seen, the father he was orange and the mother she was green," so goes the ballad made so popular by the Clancy Brothers in the 1960s. But it was certainly a direct hit on my family. Christine and Conor both stood out from their respective tribal colours, but perhaps tribal blood wins out. Teaching the politics of religion, my family background provided plenty of material.

I loved living in London, I valued my anonymity in contrast to a smaller Irish context, and the somewhat blissful indifference of most people. I always felt this to be absent in Ireland. Working in London offered the possibility of having a very wide circle of friends, not confined to university colleagues. Our network included journalists, bankers, broadcasters, business people, lawyers and writers, as well as academic colleagues. One of the reasons we moved to London from Sussex when I was diagnosed with MS was that I did not wish to be in a university town, although some tentative efforts had been made to appoint me to the Politics Department at Sussex University. I loved the big city atmosphere, where the School was only a small part.

Rita was invited to attend the World Congress of Sociology in September 1970 in Varna Bulgaria on the Black Sea. I sulked and said I would accompany her if we could visit Istanbul afterwards. We boarded a Balkan air flight in Heathrow where a great deal of commotion and confusion preceded take-off. This was only resolved when twenty pieces of luggage were loaded into the aisle of the cabin. We were terrified and hardly reassured by the buxom blondes of the cabin crew who had little or no English. I think the flight, which climbed slowly and worryingly only reached its full flying height near to Paris. We were not re-assured by a retired British pilot sitting across from us, who looked just as alarmed. We were grateful to have landed in Sofia, where my Bulgarian phrase book allowed me to order two bottle of wine at one time (<u>tva botillika</u>) - particularly important because the waiters appeared to be communist public servants, conspicuous by their absence or inactivity.

When I tried to attend some of the Congress sessions, I was turned away by well-muscled "sociologists," guardians of the gates accredited for the occasion. Following the Congress, we boarded the Orient Express, which arrived eight hours late in Sofia. The journey to Istanbul across northern Greece was about 250 miles(?). We settled down for the night and when we pulled open the curtains the following morning, we realized that the signs of the village stations we were passing at a slow pace were in Greek. There was no food on the train, apart from a large ancient samovar tended by a tired waiter in a white jacket. We arrived in Istanbul 24 hours late. But Istanbul more than made up for the tedious journey.

Rita and I enjoyed a brief winter weekend in the Netherlands when I lectured at the Institute of Social Studies in The Hague. We enjoyed the Mauritzhaus Museum and all the many ways one could serve sole in the Saar restaurant which had been recommended to us. In Amsterdam in began to snow, which made the cobbled stone streets along the canals even more magical. We walked and occasionally stopped for Genaver (Dutch gin) which served as a kind of anti-freeze against the cold. This proved to be a mistake as it was followed by an overly heavy meal in an overly heated restaurant. We were much the worse for wear the following morning.

Research in Africa as Tourism

Conor was outraged that one of the neurologists had told me to treat my MS as a "witches warning." Unbeknownst to me, Rita and Conor had discussed the possibility of trying to help me with my hesitancy of leaving London and returning to Africa. I somehow felt that I did not wish to be too far from UCH. But I agreed to consult the neurology team about this idea. It was something of an uphill struggle as I assured them that I had no intention of spending months in a insalubrious mud hut with my family. Rather, I said, we had in mind an air-conditioned villa in the diplomatic quarters of Dakar and Algiers. It was 1975 and we set off with our respective research grants. Sarah, who was six, attended a nearby primary school which was taught in French but Wolof was the language of the playground. She learned some of both. She travelled to and from school on a car rapide (crowded mammy wagon, as they call them in Ghana or Nigeria) with Emily Apter, our nanny. Emily had been the flower girl at our wedding in Berkeley, which was held in her parents' garden in the Berkeley Hills. She was now a Radcliffe graduate in English literature, but thought that being in Africa with us for six months would be a lark.

Our sometime lodger that year (in our oversized residence) was the historian, Martin Klein from the University of Toronto. I remember him as great company for all the family with a grizzled beard and a bottle of chilled Kebir Rose (Moroccan, and pretty well all that was available), with which he turned up for dinner each evening. He paid special attention to Sarah, who explained to us that she understood because he missed his own children, Moses and Elka. Martin organized a wonderful tour of the Sine Saloum region of the coast south of Dakar, where he had done research that year, mostly by dugout canoe.

We all piled into the car for a nostalgic visit to Touba and the Mourides, particularly to see my old research assistant,

Thierno Sow and his family. For many hours we sat on mats on the sand in his courtyard as his young wives platted the hair of Sarah and of Emily with small beads in the local style. I sat with him and updated my knowledge of the brotherhood, discussing particularly the changes in leadership since I left eight years before.

The most important news about the Mourides even then was how they had begun to fan out through Europe from France in large numbers, talibes (followers) organized and sent by their sheikhs in return for handsome remittances to their coffers with the remainder to their families. These bana banas or petty street traders later became ubiquitous from New York to Moscow, and not so-petty-traders as they became big business.

The Baay Fall had become even more of a morality police keeping order than they had been when we were in Touba originally on the orders of the Calif. On one subsequent visit with the family, we were arrested by some typically thuggish characters on the approach road to Touba because we had a carton of cigarettes in the car. I protested that the only force with the authority to arrest us was the local police. So they led us to the police station in the nearby town of M'Bake to meet a bemused police officer, who instructed them to leave as he would deal with it. Once they had gone, he said, we could be on our way, but advised us to hide the cigarettes.

The Baay Fall had become even more of a morality police keeping order than they had been when we were in Touba originally on the orders of the Calif. On one subsequent visit

18. At Fedelma's wedding

19. Best man at a friend's wedding

20. On Conor's Thames Houseboat

21. With Fedelma at Burgh Hill, Sussex

22. With Rita's father in France

23. Howth Summit

24. Family together in Thaxsted

25. With Conor at Wells Cathedral

26. With Nancy

27. With Sarah

28. With Sarah in Jumiege, France

originally on the orders of the Calif. On one subsequent visit with the family, we were arrested by some typically thuggish characters on the approach road to Touba because we had a carton of cigarettes in the car. I protested that the only force with the authority to arrest us was the local police. So they led us to the police station in the nearby town of M'Bake to meet a bemused police officer, who instructed them to leave as he would deal with it. Once they had gone, he said, we could be on our way, but advised us to hide the cigarettes.

In Dakar, we used to go to the beach at lunchtime and on one such occasion, Emily got out of her depth in the sea and into difficulty, waving frantically. A local fisherman started to make his way towards her, but I waved him back. I was also swimming, but in my depth and began talking soothingly to Emily, pointing out that she was already in an on-shore current. All she needed to do was to stay on her back, kicking gently. She did this, while I stayed out of arms-length, and she was soon out of danger. I later learned that Emily always remembered me as the person who saved her life.

Before we left Senegal, Rita, Sarah and I went to Casamance by steamship, heading for the Island of Carabane upstream the River Casamance. We stayed in a fairly primitive dwelling among succulent tropical palms – an eco-treat after four months in the savannah of northern Senegal. We arrived early on a Sunday morning and went to look at the old Portuguese-built church with pews disintegrating from woodworm, which clattered nosily on the stone floor when we tried to sit down. There were porcelain white Madonna images and animal droppings from the local herds, as the doors were similarly eaten away. We had arrived in time for mass. The sermon to which we were welcomed was on the subject of Doubting Thomas, more appropriate to a Paris audience than the few local villagers in attendance besides us. At breakfast each morning, the cook arrived to ask what we would like for dinner – on a strictly limited menu. Then, as we ate breakfast, she went out and chased screaming small fowl around the yard until she caught our evening meal.

Leaving Carabane, after a blissful, beautiful and quiet few days in the heart of a once Portugese ex-slave colony, we missed the motorized launch for the ship. We were carried bags and all in a dug-out canoe by two enterprising locals into the choppy river in a squall. We approached alongside several other canoes (selling local produce) bobbing up and down rather dangerously. We felt very frightened when suddenly Sarah was plucked to safety through a porthole on the ship by a large black American marine (to whom may our blessings be eternal).

We arrived in Algiers for a shorter research tour of six weeks and settled into Hydra, a beautiful suburb, high above the city. Sarah attended the local American school where the high point of her experience was a large snake in the courtyard, which was killed by the gardener. She said she did not really learn much.

A high point for me was an interview with Claudine Chaulet, a long established local sociologist, born in Algiers and married there. She had done an impressive study of self-managed agriculture (autogestion) in the fertile northern region of the Mitidja. Self-management was in those days at the heart of applied Marxist thinking. When I asked Claudine how things had been going in recent years, she made a somewhat dismissive wave, "Oh, it is simple. There are the degourdis and the abroutis. The degourdis (to use an Irish term – "lads on the make") leave the farms, while the abroutis ("knuckleheads" in American) remained because they knew no better.

A second important encounter related to my research on reformist Islam as proto-nationalism. I talked with the dashing Minister of Culture, Taleb Ibrahimi, the grandson of Cheikh Ibrahimi, an important leader of the Association of Reformist Ulema in the 1930s. Taleb had written a book on Albert Camus. I told him that my father had also done so and had felt that Camus left the Arabs out of the story out of guilt. Our conversation then took a very personal turn. Taleb had been married to a French woman and asserted that mixed marriages did not work because the two people lacked shared memories. I said, "Sometimes, they do work." And he gave a gentle shrug. On leaving I told him that he had done more for Algeria than his famous grandfather. He added with a smile that the only other person who has previous ventured that opinion had been President Boumedienne. Had I returned to Algeria, I would have greatly welcomed a further relationship with this man who is to this day still regarded as one of Algeria's foremost intellectuals.

One of the great pleasures of our stay in Algiers was being in the company of Sinclair Road, who lived in Algiers representing the UK Committee on Middle East Trade. "Tinker, Taylor, Soldier, Sinclair?" While I cherished this illusion, I think it was an unjustified suspicion. I thought, however, it added a little spice to our acquaintance. Sinclair was very generous with his time and his resources and treated us to fine meals in town. He drove us in his comfortable Citroen DS through the mountains of Kabila en route to a most stylish new hotel – so new that the road up to it had yet to be built. We were the only guests and it felt like a bizarre film – another triumph of Rita's frontier tourism. Sinclair entertained us with stories his travels and his career. He told us that he never learned Arabic because then you were certainly considered a spy.

Our last trip in Algeria took us deep into the Sahara by air to the ancient oasis used in trans-desert trade, Ghardhia. Here we stayed in the Hotel "Transat," owned by an old French couple with an overgrown tropical garden (during French rule, an outlying post of the steamship company, Transatlantique). En route from the airport by car, we were flanked by camel-driving Toureg in pale blue flowing robes and white headgear. We called to Sarah to look at the spectacle, as she turned very briefly from her French Pif comic. Her finest moment was in the hotel swimming pool. Sarah was just learning the swim, but she could do an impressive job of treading water. She managed to cross the pool treading backwards, observed by two tough –looking Frenchmen who took their cigarettes from their mouths, as one remarked," Ca, c'est réellement pas mal!" I felt as if I'd had a slap on the back, too.

In all our fairly entertaining travel that year, it may be remarked that MS has not even had a mention. There were some slight symptoms during these months, but nothing to be concerned about. This was encouragement to me and even more so to my principal backers. Rita and Conor were not going to let me get away with hiding behind my medical incapacities. Life could still be a lot of fun.

CHAPTER 9

The Family, Academic Projects and Travels Abroad

Maybe it's because I'm a Dubliner that I love London so

My mother seemed rather sad about the infrequency of my visits to Dublin. It is true that I limited those stays to three days, enough time to see each of my sisters and my parents at home, but not enough time for anything else. Christine's circle was exclusively local. I felt that she would have wished me to have stayed in Dublin, while I was intent on running in the other direction. All the same, I did feel nostalgia for the coconut aroma of the gorse bushes near my father's home.

In my quest to distance myself from Dublin, I am reminded of an American song, "Wildcat Kelley," written by Cole Porter in 1934, which I always loved:

> *Oh, give me land, lots of land under starry skies above*
> *Don't fence me in.*
> *Let me ride through the wide open country that I love*
> *Don't fence me in.*
>
> *Let me be by myself in the evenin' breeze*

And listen to the murmur of the cottonwood trees
Send me off forever but I ask you please
Don't fence me in!

My attempt to claim my independence from Dublin and family were different to my sisters, Kate and Fedelma. It really started long years before when my parents were in Paris. The girls were taken out of the local French school after two terms when Kate was injured. Fedelma remained at home to keep her company and they never returned. Christine was pretty depressed at the time about her relationship to Conor, and the house by the river in La Frette sur Seine became something of a refuge for discontented women. I observed this and it reverberated several years later when I still felt that my sisters were held in Christine's comfortable orbit and not allowed the freedom to seek their own way in life. My observation provoked a confrontation with Christine and George and a vigorous denial. There was for many years a distinct coolness in our relationship.

Kate had a close English friend at Trinity; they were inseparable and she was closely guarded from contact with the rest of the family. As Kate's career developed into writing and editorial work for a publisher, she went on to encourage many young Irish authors. As an accomplished writer herself, who initially wrote principally about the family, she struggled to make her voice heard and could understand young author's well. She subsequently enjoyed many personal tributes for her encouragement.

You could describe my relationship with Kate as always having been rather fraught. We maintained a rather cautious connection. I treasure the memory of a walk with Kate when she took me aside, a few months before she died in 1989. She told me that she regretted that we had remained sparring partners for so long, since we had much in common as fellow writers.

When Kate died suddenly of a brain haemorrhage at the age of 50, Conor's immediate reaction was to say that it was not a bad way to go. But for weeks, perhaps months thereafter he would walk into the front garden overlooking the sea in light or darkness and howl. He was reticent when people tried to comfort him and persuade him to return inside. His grief was strong, but we never actually discussed it and he left us all to make our own way with it.

Fedelma had a network exclusively in Dublin. Her friends were interesting and thoughtful people, starting with girls from Park House School. Fedelma married the son of a Protestant cleric who became the Archbishop of all Ireland. Her career included the management of the Oxfam shop in Rathmines, where she lives, for a long time the most successful one in Ireland.

Conor was very much a Dubliner, but had unpredictable movements – as much at ease travelling which he greatly enjoyed as being at home. My visits with him were usually great fun. Walks on the hill of Howth - he with his walking stick, which had once belonged to Charles Parnell. He loved his home on the summit, especially the spectacular view, thirty miles of the Irish east coast as far as Wicklow Head. On a fine day in the early morning, the coast of Wales was often visible. Patrick and Margaret, young adolescents by now, had an exuberant life with their friends on the summit and in and out of the house. Our daughter, Sarah, began a close relationship with Margaret which lasts until this day.

Rita resented having to spend our time in Dublin exclusively with the family. But I had no interest in doing other things or meeting other people. The truth is I couldn't wait to get back to London. Neither of my parents had anything like a home in which I felt altogether comfortable. Perhaps they all breathed a sigh of relief when I left to return to London. It was from there that I was to head off to various places in the coming years.

Ah les beaux jours!

A choice destination was to be with Cecilia Gillie in her French village, Mirabeau, in the Vaucluse. We went there every summer from the mid- seventies. The weather was one attraction; the food another, but most of all it was Cecilia's warm, welcoming presence. Her kitchen was the centre of our social life, chatting and chopping, a little local wine on the counter – always the same - a watery litre of Cote du Luberon which suited the hot evenings. Talk on any subject, particularly the new recipes for Cecilia's cookbook which was in preparation, or hearing stories of the wayward life of the war years in London, political corruption in France…..and then refill the glasses. Cecilia also flattered me about my attitude towards MS. Her own resilient and tough attitude to life impressed me in return. But we tried our best not to be an unbearable mutual admiration society.

Mirabeau stands perched in the foothills of the Luberon Mountains, a spectacularly beautiful site where we found plenty to do within a few kilometres of the village. On hot summer days we would close the shutters of the house and head off to the nearby Etang de la Bonde where we could swim, read, chat and enjoy pain bagna (open sandwiches) in the heat of the day.

There was one year when Rita's sister Nancy came to stay with a project that we should all go down to the Cote d'Azur. As we usually liked to remain in our village backwater during August far away from the crowds on the coast, there was some initial consternation, particularly about the cost of finding last minute accommodation. Nancy's project was rescued by neighbours who were ready to help out with the loan of a large family tent and associated equipment. We arrived at a camp site on the edge of Antibes and got the last available site on a sun-baked small hill where the ground to had turned to cement. Our tent was a very elaborate affair with an awning, kitchen and two double bedrooms. We struggled with this mighty holiday home – or should I say that the three women in my family did, while I sat in a deck chair nearby giving orders under a large sun hat. The labourers protested that I was like a colonial officer with his natives, offering incompetent advice. They "manfully" finally got the crucial four perimeter pegs into the ground after considerable effort.

We showered and headed off to Antibes for dinner. We staggered home and tucked up into our sleeping bags. In the middle of the night the worst summer storm of the season descended and created a river of rushing water under the tent. I woke to see Nancy doing her best to gather up the kitchen equipment which had clattered to the ground noisily waking up the French families in the adjacent tents. They were particularly scathing in their remarks about our incompetence and about foreigners, as well. The local newspapers reported the flooding the next day. We headed off to Nice under grey skies and felt that we had done the Cote d'Azur once and forever.

In 1976 Cecilia was trying to make up her mind whether to remain in Provence in her beautiful home and garden or return to England, following the death of her husband. We offered to be with her while she considered that choice. We stumbled on a top-mark boondoggle: the Euro-scholar scheme. Rita and I applied to the Centre de Recherches et d'Etudes sur les Societes Magribin (CRESM) where we proposed to continue the research we had started in Algeria the year before.

The Director of CRESM was a pillar of the local establishment, true Mediterranean man. He was an excellent host and ready for a laugh on any occasion, preferably assisted by a good supply of local wine. The other principal star of CRESM was from a prominent Norman family, austere in style and with an American post-graduate degree, a much more rigorous mainstream political scientist. The institutional life of

CRESM was largely based on trying to reconcile these two different styles and their respective entourages. As visitors, we were in a good position to keep out of harm's way, expressing our enthusiastic support for the life style of one and the scholarship of the other.

The person who perhaps got the most out of our stay in Mirabeau was Sarah. She was enrolled in the village school with the little French she had learned in Dakar and she thrived. The schoolmistress, following the prevalent tradition which remained in French schools at this time frequently resorted to corporal punishment which horrified Sarah. As a visiting English child she was well out of the firing line, but Jean Cristophe was not so lucky. We often had Sarah's teacher to tea before we were aware of any of this. Sarah always remained at school for lunch even if we were in the village a few hundred yards away, as she never wanted to miss Mme. Michel's frites which were cooked for the children every day with their midday meal.

By the end of our stay Cecilia was able to tell us that she had made her decision to remain in Mirabeau. The explanation was all around us, a little corner of paradise set against the alternative of returning to England where she had fewer close companions of her generation any longer and little enough draw in climatic terms. She flattered us by sharing her decision with us before telling her relatives and friends in England.

The Franco-British Research Project

The best promotion there ever was came in 1983. I was appointed a Reader in Political Studies (with reference to Africa) – a promotion which left the way open to becoming a professor in due course. This promotion was a recognition of Saints and Politicians (1975) which was well reviewed.

In 1980 and 82, SOAS hosted conferences on Islam and Politics in Sub-Saharan Africa. During the second conference, together with Christian Coulon, Director of the Institute of African Studies in Bordeaux, we recognized that it might be a good idea to launch a joint project. At the time, Islam was already a matter of policy concern in governing and academic circles. We approached the respective research councils of the UK and France and were successful. Coulon and I became joint directors of a team of nine scholars who worked together from 1983-89. Christian and I ruefully acknowledged at our first meeting that there was a somewhat marginal relationship of either of us to the national labels of our Franco-British project. He thought of himself as more Gascon than French and I, as Irish, was also somewhat marginal, but, in truth, I think by then, I felt a bit more British than Irish.

Our good fortune in having Bordeaux as the location of our French meetings was gastronomic as well as intellectual. Early on, Christian took me on a tour of the Médoc where we visited the celebrated vineyards of Leoville Lascaze and Beycheville, not to speak of his own small vineyard worked by his charming parents at La Marque. The Coulons had had a long career as well-known charcutiers in Bordeaux and there the family tradition of excellent cuisine was established. Our French counterparts found cooking and drinking wine an inexhaustible subject – where to get the best ingredients, how to cook and present the best ingredients and the best vintage to accompany the meal.

Charisma was the subject of the first collaborative volume for which I wrote the introduction. It opened with the words, "In the beginning was the miracle. Muslim leaders dealt with in this volume, African saints of the past two hundred years, were all credited with miraculous achievements at decisive moments in their exercise of leadership. The miracle was indeed to be seen as the decisive credential in an Islamic power-play." It was published as Charisma and Brotherhood in African Islam in 1988.

The second volume of our research was to have been on Islam and the state in post-colonial Africa. We discussed the instability of the states with which we were dealing. One of the main themes was how state entities tried to incorporate the youth of cities who were unemployed, reluctant to follow their elders and looking overseas for a viable future. We discussed how the brotherhoods related to the political system and in some cases added to state legitimacy.

The contributions were prepared and ours were translated into French, as the second volume was to be published in France. Everything was in hand, but Christian seemed unable to write the introduction or supervise the publication and the volume never saw the light of day. Looking back on it now I feel that I should have gone ahead and written the introduction myself, enabling it to be published. I think all the colleagues would have welcomed my doing so, but I held back in a diplomatic way, perhaps behaving like an Irishman's idea of a true Englishman. The contributions were returned to each author and published elsewhere. This was a great personal disappointment with a close colleague with whom I worked and of course it left the commitment of the grant unfulfilled. I was very angry and brooded over it for a long time.

My travels to France led me to become acquainted with the poor access provided for disabled people. On one occasion when travelling to Bordeaux, I stayed in the flat of a friend on the Boulevard Raspail in Paris. I arrived from London after dark in a heavy rainfall and parked my car, carefully displaying the disabled badge on the windscreen and headed off to bed. The following morning, the car was not there. A notice pinned to a lamppost informed me that the car could be found in the police station in Montparnasse, where I would be charged the appropriate fine. I had begun to use a scooter to get around, as my limp had turned into a hobble by then.

I drove it to the police station indicated and sought out the officer in charge. She gave me a respectful look when she realized that I had travelled a mile in my scooter to search for the car. She examined the notice I was carrying and looked at me and said, "This is an outrage. It should never have happened." My crime was that the disabled badge was not French. She released the car with no charge, having treated me with immense respect for getting around on my own. At that time, I was told by a Parisian friend to whom I complained about the absence of dropped pavements for strolling along the quais of the Seine, that most people in wheelchairs in France stayed at home.

On a subsequent holiday in Paris, I had another encounter with the French state about the issue of access. We found ourselves trapped in the underground car park in the front of Notre Dame Cathedral, unable to exit except by a busy entry ramp. I wrote to Mayor Jacques Chirac about this incident and others, including the lack of access to museums in Paris. I received a reply from the Mayor's Assistant on Handicapped Affairs. He assured me that the Mayor had my problems in mind and that my "integration into life" was one of his major priorities. Top marks, I thought, for French insolence.

Gaddafi, the Tortoise

Rita and I had an early spring holiday in Tunisia around this time. We had originally thought of driving around Normandy, but as it was March, we decided to head for the sun. Only it rained every single day on the sea coast in Hammamet and Rita had finished reading Ernest Jones lengthy biography of Sigmund Freud and I, three volumes of Stephen Runcimen's, History of the Crusades. We decided to head for Tunis and visited with friends - Souad and Abdelkader Zghal. She was the most gracious of hostesses; and he was an exceedingly amusing sociologist. One day out walking on a vacant lot near their home, we came upon a tortoise about the size of a man's hand. Abdelkader picked it up and said, "You must take this home to Sarah."

At the time, Mumar Gaddafi was making his first state visit to Tunisia, his reputation and antics became a source of great amusement to sophisticated Tunis residents who regarded him as an uncivilized apparition from the desert. Abdelkader said, "We shall call him Gaddafi...". He had a painted yellow shell, which we cleaned with a toothbrush. Rita carried the live contraband through Luton airport in a plastic bag, while I walked ahead ignoring her in fear of her imminent apprehension for importing a live animal.

When we got safely home, Rita rang the RSPCA and asked for the tortoise specialist, who was pleased but also amazed that we had been in touch, to ask how to care for the new pet. Very few people did and most of the small beasts died within a few years. He asked for his description and measurements and announced that his genus was Libyan to our surprise. We were told that we needed to have him hibernate every winter in a dry cold place, and we managed to keep him for about ten years in a box of straw in the old coal storage place under the basement steps. We placed him there when the weather got cold and to our amazement would hear him scratching around in the box in spring.

Gaddafi loved to eat barbecued chicken bones, so summers were a good feed for him. He also liked fresh peas and nibbling people's toes if they wore sandals. Odd that, as tortoises is supposed to be vegetarian. But not him. He survived an attack from a friend's Jack Russell which left a chip in his shell. Several years after he joined our household, a visiting Parisian leftist academic charged us with disrespect at naming a household pet after an African head of state. Our answer to this charge is that he had been named by a Tunisian. Gaddafi survived until our move to Hampstead. He swallowed a slug pellet in the garden during the chaos of moving day. We buried him in the garden with a small memorial which survived many years. He had a more dignified end than his namesake.

Academic Projects and Travels Abroad

In 1978, I was a Truman Fellow at the Institute of International Affairs in Jerusalem. Rita, Sarah and I lived in a university flat on Mt. Scopus, which prior to the 1967 was occupied by the UN as disputed territory. Our neighbour was Professor Michael Handel who was an expert on international security issues and took a "tough guy" stand for Israel. More congenial company were the old distinguished scholars at the Hebrew University including some famous social scientists to whom we had introductions. This generation retained the hospitable approach to visitors which had been typical of the Jewish Diaspora. I found my colleagues at the Institute, all of whom were sabras, to be typical of the younger generation of Israelis who were interesting but tough and brusque. When we returned to London I mentioned this generational contrast to my Iraqi colleague, Abbas Kelidar, who said that the sabras were reacting against what they considered to be the servile good manners of the ghetto. Perhaps…

In January 1979 Conor became Editor in Chief of The Observer and we saw a great deal more of him. He lived on a houseboat at Chelsea Reach once the Special Branch decided that it was safe for him to do so. He returned to Dublin at the weekends when we used the boat, including several birthday parties for Sarah and pleasant weekends with friends. In 1984 we moved from our four story early Victorian house in Islington to a garden flat in Hampstead. Although I loved the house with its roof garden and wonderful roses, the steps had become very difficult for me. We had looked into the possibility of installing a lift, but the house was very narrow and it was not feasible.

In November 1988, I was invited to a state dinner at Buckingham Palace in honour of the President of Senegal, Abdou Diouf. The event was an expression of national gratitude for the use of Dakar airport as a refuelling stop for the RAF during the Falklands War. This was a courageous stance on his part and contrary to almost all developing countries and France at the time…well worth a fancy dinner. We dined on gold plates and shared a footman in service. The grand occasion was completed when leaving the palace - being waved into the traffic by the guards, only to instantly regain our status as ordinary folk. I attended with Sarah as on the same night Rita was opening a rather splendid bar and restaurant in Soho: "Mitchell and O'Brien," based on a New York Deli.

In this period I made two visits to Senegal on my own: one for a conference at the University and the other for the US State

29. Boating on Cape Cod

30. On the ferry from Dublin

31. Boating, Cape Cod

32. Lunch in Provence

33. Mt. Blanc

34. Sailing in Provincetown, Mass.

35. Picnic near Mirabeau, France

36. Nephews Laurence and Alexander

37. With Cecilia Gillie

38. The gents at Sarah's wedding

39. Sarah's wedding

40. In conversation with Kate and nephew, Mark

Department who were interested in gaining insight into the brotherhood leaders in Senegal. I was particularly pleased that I was able to make the journeys and local travels on my own with the assistance of others and my scooter. Reflecting on the ethics of working for the State Department, it must have been an indicator of my modified political views with advancing years, as I would never have contemplated informing the US government about Senegal when I did my initial research as a much younger man. In California terminology, I had become a "fink."

My final publication prior to retirement was <u>Staging Politics: Power and Performance in Asia and Africa</u>, published in 2007, co-edited with my colleague, Julia Strauss. For a number of years, Julia and I had jointly taught the State and Society course at SOAS, a great pleasure to me. We found that better students year after year, were attracted to the idea of politics as theatre. We decided to mount a small international conference on the subject as a prelude to further possible comparative research. The book began with a description of the performative – including ritual and theatre together with more common institutional and interest based approaches.

Rita was working at London Business School and was the Director of their mid-career MBA programme which included an annual module in Hong King and China. On the third and last time when she was going to make the trip, she asked me to join her, saying that our accommodation would be paid for by the programme. I was touched that she had asked me, and nonplussed when within a day of two she added the little rider that it would of course be helpful if I could pay for my air travel. Nothing ventured; nothing gained, I made a request to the Nuffield Foundation. I informed them that it would be a trip around many corners of Asia with all hotel costs covered, only the air transport to be paid business class, on grounds of disability.

The purpose of my visit was to talk to people in Shanghai and Delhi on the subject of the local understanding of democracy: what did democracy mean in these two locations? In Shanghai, I arrived at Fu Dan University in my wheelchair to be faced with a long flight of steps which was typical of the lack of facilities in public places for the disabled in Chinese cities. I told the party which greeted me that either we had the discussion where I sat outside the building or they would have to carry my wheelchair down the flight of steps. They were diffident about this, perhaps reflecting on the past life of Chinese coolies, but in the end they relented. When I arrived at the seminar, there were no apparent students in attendance, so I asked "Where are the students?" and the Professor replied, "Students do not understand about democracy."

We enjoyed walking on the Bund in Shanghai, reflecting on how closely it resembled the waterfront in Liverpool, which was hardly an accident since it was the same generation of British architects who had designed both. We marvelled at the early days of "the Manhattan of Asia," across the river in Pudong, which today has many more spectacular skyscrapers than its model. One evening we were taken to an astonishing spectacle in a somewhat seedy hotel where a small group of

Chinese entertainers of a certain age were singing Pat Boone songs with wonderfully accurate diction and tone. These guys had somehow managed to maintain this pastime during the Cultural Revolution with low voices and drawn curtains. Their rendition was perfect but we discovered when we joined them afterwards that they really did not speak a word of English. China was an adventure in a wheelchair, particularly as we were chased at the entrance to the Forbidden City in Beijing with wild gesticulations and a lot of shouting we did not understand, but seemed to indicate that vehicles were prohibited. But we managed.

The next stop on our Eastern journey was Bangkok where we stayed at the Oriental Hotel which must be luxury's own lap. Rita organized a boat for me to tour the river, the best way to see the spectacular temples, the greatest feature of the city. The large boat could accommodate 40 but turned out to be the only way that one in a wheelchair could see the river in comfort. I remember the smile of one of the hotel staff, a beautiful smile of regret that we would only spend one day in the city.

We travelled to Hanoi to stay with a friend who was the Swedish ambassador and his wife. Keeping up the motif of luxury, we headed off for Halong Bay, a great natural site, in his chauffeured Mercedes. I had the eerie feeling of having seen the location in the French film, "Indochine". It was misty but we enjoyed a solo boat trip again around the bay. Back on dry land, the city of Hanoi contained various presences, from French colonial style to the all pervasive beginnings of capitalism. The French and the Americans may have lost the war in Viet Nam, but that wasn't stopping capitalism and the reaction to all this was one of local exuberance, a lot of style, and personal self-expression notably in the choice of amazing hats.

If students would not understand democracy in Shanghai, the same certainly did not hold true for students in Delhi. The high point of my tour in terms of the Nuffield funded enquiry was the Centre for Electoral Studies at Jawaharlal Nehru University. Yogendra Yadav was my host and guide during several very fruitful days. The question at the back of my mind was how far democracy could accommodate such a huge pile of problems from ethnic to religious and from caste to class. Yogendra convinced me that there wasn't anything else that could do the job – authoritarianism having had a go under Mrs. Ghandi to no great effect.

While we were in India, we did not neglect touring and again (under the disabled heading) went about as far as one could go. We travelled to Agra by car and on Christmas Eve found ourselves in the spectacular 17th century fort of Fatipur Sikri, where I was able to visit every courtyard and building thanks to being carried in my push wheelchair by teams of four people. Later similar visits to Jain temples near Udaipur were impressive. People carried on with their devotions as I was being hauled around all the halls and alters.

Our last stop on this six week tour of Asia was the Lake Palace Hotel in Udaipur, which was actually in the middle of a lake, an achieved fantasy of an 18th century Maharana (local ruler). We sat there reflecting on our recent travels coming to the conclusion that we would never be able to beat them. We concluded that it was therefore time to think of getting a place in the country back in England where we could live on the memories. At the New Year's Eve celebrations in the hotel, I recall the current Maharana sitting in the corner of the festivities looking rather bored in paradise.

We spend summer holidays thereafter for several years on the Beara Peninsula in Kerry. We enjoyed successive waves of family visitors from Dublin. We were on the lookout for a place to buy and had things pinned down to a particular area on the Kenmare River. I was always more reticent than Rita as far as this quest was concerned. She enjoyed the status of being the wife of a returning son, but the son resisted the idea of returning. Finally I said to her: "I want to get in the car in Hampstead and get out at the other end." That put pay to the Irish project.

The trigger to our resolve was a holiday in Normandy and the Loire with Rita's father and his partner. When we returned from hosting and driving them around the French countryside, we decided most emphatically that it was time to do something for ourselves. And so we did. We set out for Dorset and after a rainy morning looking at totally unsuitable thatched cottages, we found a timber house which reminded us of California in the window of an estate agent in Dorchester and decided to buy it that day. It was September 1998 when we moved in.

Country Life in Dorset and Family Matters

We settled into country life, enjoying Dorset, developing the garden, creating a wildlife pond. We also built a conservatory with my retirement lump sum, an excellent investment. It was a time to get to know the people in the village and our neighbours, in particular Daniel, the next door neighbour – a 30 year old fish and chips entrepreneur with a garden of wonderful tropical plants and a young family. Our local squire, from the only estate in the village was Martin Cree. Our first encounter was a negotiation about cutting the hedge between our properties. That was when I discovered that he had roots in County Clare, of which he was greatly proud. Snap. He was a quintessential Englishman (Sherborne and Balliol) but we greatly enjoyed sharing stories about our respective ancestors from the same county. To enjoy the countryside, I purchased a robust large scooter to do the challenging walks along the coast. Much of these lands have been in the custody of the Ministry of Defence since the Second World War who protect the flora and fauna, and among others, the skylarks.

Our daughter, Sarah, chose San Francisco as the location for her marriage to Jamie Latham in 2003. She explained the choice of venue in a national park on the coast across the Golden Gate Bridge partly on the basis that they did not wish to have a big wedding in London. It was then fashionable to go to exotic places in distant locations and Sarah found this particular location on a website called, "weddings by the bay.com" which even provided a pastor for the ceremony.

There was also a sentimental consideration, reflecting back to our own wedding in the area. A pre-wedding party was hosted by Rita's cousin, Jules Heumann, who had done the same for us in his spectacular home on one of the San Francisco's peaks, overlooking the whole area. It was very hard to be unsentimental on this occasion. We enjoyed a reception on a yacht in the harbour.

Joe was born in 2005 followed by Lily, three years later. Jamie and Sarah have continued to work on the creative side of advertising. Sarah works part time in a local agency and Jamie, in London. They live in St. Albans, Hertfordshire, twenty miles north of London, a town with a great sense of its own history, excellent schools and many young families. Joe and Lily are now in school and Joe has started playing rugby, much to my delight. Recently his (young) Old Albanian Team won the country championships for the under sevens. Lily is a very exuberant child who loves books, school and dressing up. Joe sometimes sees himself as Lily's teacher, while Lily is a good deal more reserved about this.

Getting real: the need to divide up the spoils

A conversation with my mother in the last years of her life touched on the subject of inheritance, a possibly troublesome area. Christine said that she had already discussed it with her husband, George, who said initially that they did not really need to be specific about items in their legacy since the family "would sort it all out." Christine had been firm with him: "Oh yes, you do need to sort it out. You must read Balzac and come back to me." He did and they earmarked every last painting and statue following that conversation; the family did not even have to talk to one another.

From about 2005 after a period of hospitalization, Conor - by then nearing ninety, began to decline. No token of decline could have been clearer than his beginning to leave a glass of wine untouched on the table in front of him at dinner; his resolve was displayed disapprovingly though if anyone tried to remove the glass. He did not want to drink it, but he would be damned if he would let anyone take it away from him. At this time, he did not take much part in conversation, but did cleave the air with his view on some person or issue when he could summon up the strength to do so.

Events in Northern Ireland at this time were moving very swiftly to apparent resolution. My nephew, Laurence, an observer for the Dublin government at crucial peace process talks witnessed a weighty moment. This was when the Reverend Ian Paisley, of an age by then, was struggling to get up from his chair at a meeting with Catholic counterparts. As he rose, seeing the difficulty, Martin McGuinness lent down to assist the old man by gently propping up his elbow. The little hairs on Lawrence's neck rose as he witnessed this site, he told me.

Given his previous position and particularly his prominent membership in the United Kingdom Unionist Party, Conor, we feared, would find these events leading toward the peaceful resolution of problems in the North very difficult to accept. At first he did. Our whispered family considerations reminded me of a film I greatly enjoyed. Made in East Germany, "Goodbye Lenin" was the story of an elderly woman living in East Berlin who had been a fervent communist. But Germany had been united and the new Berlin was changing rapidly around her. Her daughter and son decided that the radical changes in the real world would be too much for her in her last few years and resolved to simulate a world for her as if the wall had not fallen and the new capitalist economy did not exist. It was a touching and humorous exercise: the Conor that might have been.

Following all this bemused family consideration, Conor was nonetheless aware of events in the North from the television news. He said that the coming together in the North was something he never thought possible. Sensing the great difficulty Conor would have had coming to terms with events, I wrote him a letter in sympathy on the eve of his 90th birthday. The letter tried to explain why I felt there had been a coming together and suggesting that Conor himself in his life career had been an important agent of that coming together. First there was his marriage to Christine and his close relationship with her father, Alec, both Presbyterians from the North. Second was his marriage to Máire and is relationship to her father, a Fianna Fail politician who took part in the 1916 rebellion and served for many years as Vice President of Ireland under De Valera. He wrote about this in this personal memoire, States of Ireland. In these two men he had good tutors, I wrote, and lots of opportunity to have learned about coming together. So many writers come from outside the North and dealt with the issues in lazy caricatures (a kind of contempt), yet you could, I wrote, take the subject seriously and offer a respectful analysis of Protestant Ulster. "Coming together with respect - both personal and political".

Conor thanked me for the letter and said that this and previous letters I had written to him had helped him remain alive in difficult times. He was referring principally to the letter, "Staying alive in Ireland." But I had also written to him about this time trying to keep him going physically. I told him that looking forward to 90 was a respectable score, but that he had also mentioned a century. If he followed my advice, I added, he would have a better chance of getting there and have more fun along the way. On the basis of my long experience of dealing with illness, I detailed a series of daily exercises and other activities for him, including the acquisition of a walking frame. I urged him to continue walking daily, however limited it might be. Prior to writing the letter I had suggested some of these things to him personally and could see from his reaction that he probably would do nothing. And so it was.

Conor had celebrated his landmark birthday with family and friends. Rita and Fedelma's husband, Nicholas organized an informal volume of tributes to him from people in Ireland, Britain and America. Some contributors had been colleagues on The Observer or shared political or academic posts with him and were delighted to hear that he had made his 90th birthday. This was printed with the cover picturing a bottle of red wine with an image of Whitewater on the label, done by our son in-law, Jamie. It contained many memorable photographs, poetry and reminiscences.

By the time Conor reached his 91st birthday, his decline called for a more muted affair. We travelled to see him: it was the last time. He died on 28 December 2008. Patrick and I both addressed the congregation. The priest who did the tribute at the service had been my PhD student, Patrick Claffey, whom I had introduced to the family. He paid many memorable visits to Maire and Conor, who particularly enjoyed his stories from Africa, collected and passed on with suitable imitation from memories of his days as a priest in Benin and Togo.

In September 2010, we moved to a flat on the Thames in Bermondsey after twenty six years residence in Hampstead. Although Hampstead had its many charms, for me it also had many steps. When we decided to move to the river, we looked for a completely accessible modern building with a lift which had a wonderful view of the river from St. Pauls to Canary Wharf. Unfortunately the first year of our south London residence found me in several different hospitals having to deal with a considerable downturn in my condition, owing to the progressive MS.

In February 2012 long after I had retired, the Politics Department at the School celebrated its 50th anniversary. At the event, two of my colleagues called attention to my early contribution to the department teaching and research. I was deeply touched that they singled me out for a great many complimentary remarks, followed by a very hearty round of applause from the floor.

Prior to this in 2005 when Christine was dying of oesophageal cancer we visited her in the Blackrock Clinic and she and I got into a close conversation. There was a glint in her eye during an amusing exchange about the family. My mother never used profane language in her entire life: it was not her style. We definitely found ourselves on a single wave length eyeball to eyeball. She blurted out, "They fuck you up, your mum and dad," (Philip Larkin). And I retorted, "He called that his Lake Isle of Innishfree," (W.B. Yeats) at which Christine dissolved in mirth. She died a few weeks later, perhaps still laughing.

41. Dorset, July 2010 birthday with Sarah, Joe and Lily

APPENDIX

Stories for Sarah

Dad could weave the most magical stories from thin air. Often he'd have to stretch the story way beyond its natural end, because of a giggling, demanding daughter. His characters were old familiar friends that filled the room, my favourite was 'Silly Bum Bum' a small schoolboy who was constantly getting into scrapes and seemed to permanently be in knee length shorts.

Unfortunately Silly Bum Bum never made it on to paper, but has always stayed with me. Storytelling is the best skill of all, and it's a tradition that lives on with Joe and Lily, a great legacy of dads. His many other charismatic characters included 'Wilber the Whale' and another firm favourite, 'Polo Bear'. Luckily mum discovered a clutch of yellowing notepaper with dad's handwriting entitled, 'The Travels of Polo Bear' and 'Wilber Whale and the Mystery Ship'.

In hospital, his good friend Mary asked dad, "What next?" once he'd finished his memoirs, and he replied, "A children's book." Mary's jaw dropped, it was a surprise to her. Dad was a great academic, but he was also a great storyteller and had a real empathy with younger readers.

On a selfish note I feel very privileged to have been the audience of one, but would have been happy to share his characters with the World. His storytelling was a gift and something I'm very thankful for, as his stories will always live on in my imagination.

The Travels of Polo Bear

Polo bear lived a quiet life at the North Pole, in his bear igloo (where he received friends, had <u>quiet</u> parties, and mostly just <u>slept</u> – very noisily, but who was there to complain about that? When he was awake, he went out fishing, through holes in the ice, gossiped with penguins and seals, and began to rub his eyes and doze until his friends would take him home (often they had to drag him across the ice by his toe nails, fast asleep). Polo was a very lazy bear, but happy enough in his way, UNTIL…

New things began to happen which were to change his whole life. Strange animals came who looked a bit like polar bears…but came in coats of all sorts of colours (which they would take off and change!) and brought all sorts of amazing things with them – funny igloos which they put up and took down, sliding carriages pulled by strange brown animals, and long sticks with pieces of coloured cloth on the end. These animals all planted their sticks, with different colours, at the same place. Then they would dance about, hug each other, and go away again after drinking a lot of stuff out of glass bottles. Very strange to a quiet polar bear.

Soon there were more than twenty flags, all at the same place. From listening behind an iceberg, Polo bear soon realised that they called it the NORTH POLE, although why they got so excited about it he still could not understand. The place looked like any other piece of ice, flat, white, and cold. Maybe Polo never would have understood, unless one of these strangers hadn't left behind a magic talking box along with a pile of empty bottles (well not quite empty, Polo found that out too). By fiddling about with this box on long, quiet nights Polo (who was a very clever bear) soon learned to talk the different languages of his visitors.

And all that he heard through his box made him curious about far-away lands and the animals who could do magic things. He decided that life at the North Pole must be <u>dull</u> compared to all of this, and that he would have to travel himself and be the first polar bear to discover the World. So he shook paws with his friends and set off, following the tracks of his latest visitors. The penguins were very sad to see him go, and Poleen wept for days and days. But Polo was a very brave bear, and excited to think of all the lands he would discover.

Where next?
This is sadly where it ends, but from dad's notes it's clear he intended to take Polo on a World tour, with outlines for chapters on Canada, Russia, China and the USA. Polo would have been a well-travelled bear, like dad he had a huge appetite to discover new places, even in his fur coat I'm sure he would have made it to Africa.

In dad's notes we also found Wilber the Whale, which was written and recorded for mum's birthday one year.

Wilber Whale and the Mystery Ship

It's hard for us to introduce Wilber to you – he is so BIG – and hard to get a picture of him down on a sheet of paper. But even though he would make you look small if you met him, and though he would not fit easily into your house, HE FELT very small, living all alone in the vasty deep of the dark ocean. Small and lonely too often enough, and maybe bored (though he never complained) THAT IS until the day when the strange undersea ship came to visit him just as he was finishing his plankton breakfast.

It was the light he saw first, far off, red and green, and the humming noise he heard growing louder as the strange vessel approached. Bigger than a whale! Yes, but clumsier maybe and certainly much <u>noisier</u>. That is, until it stopped, quite close to where Wilber was silently waiting – what was he waiting for? We don't know, but he was an inquisitive whale as well as a brave one – maybe foolish you might think, since he did know that these noisy vessels were often very bad news for whales. But Wilber had never seen whales hunted by undersea vessels – somehow he didn't believe in that – and his curiosity told him to wait and watch.

And he was rewarded for his silent wait. Two small and very clumsy looking creatures crawled out of the top of the strange vessel, attached to lines, and they began to drop towards the ocean floor. And then the vessel shined a very powerful light on the seabed as the two figures landed. What were they looking for? Wilber couldn't imagine – maybe they were hungry for lobsters? He just <u>had</u> to find out.

When the two creatures landed on the seabed, they began to walk about in the clumsiest way, poking around them, turning over stones, pulling from time to time on their lines. They seemed to get more and more discouraged, slower moving, it seemed a long time, UNTIL SUDDENLY, when they turned over a long flat stone, the two clumsy creatures seemed to go mad with joy. Why? Wilber didn't know, but they poked each other, they tugged frantically on their lines and they looked up towards their vessel (shielding their eyes from the very bright light) and one of them picked up the long flat object. The other one took a very strong pull on the line (he almost fell over). Then they both began to rise from the seabed, pulled upward towards their vessel while one of them hugged the flat shape close.

What happened then? We don't know exactly, Wilber stayed as still as he could, watching, but maybe he did gawp just a little bit in his excitement. Wouldn't you? Anyway it seems that the strange creatures suddenly noticed Wilber, they pointed at him and waved (not friendly waves, Wilber didn't think) they got so excited (frightened?) that they dropped the box (it was a box, Wilber could see that now) and it fell down to the seabed without the strange creatures paying it any further notice. All they seemed to want now was to get back to their vessel, and up they went.

Wilber hadn't lost interest in the flat box, not at all. He had noticed, when it hit the seabed, that it had split, and Wilber could have sworn that he saw a glint of yellow? He could safely find out about all of that soon enough, as the undersea vessel was leaving, no whale could have known where for.

What does a whale do with a flat box? Hard to know, and Wilber certainly wasn't as excited about the box as the two clumsy creatures seemed to have been. Maybe you could store lobsters in the box? But whales don't eat lobsters, and the box would be no use for storing plankton (they would leak out through the cracks in the wood). Still there must be something a whale can do with a flat box. Wilber hated to be thought of as stupid (even though there was nobody near in the vasty ocean to mock him or call him a whale-brain) and he saw that box as a challenge to his mighty intelligence. What to do?

The first thing was to take a good look at the mystery box close up. That's what Wilber thought anyway, he couldn't think of a better idea. Can you?... So down he dived to the seabed. He touched the box gently with his tail — at least he thought he was being gentle, though the box did split open. Out of it spilled some bright yellow metal objects. They didn't mean a thing to Wilber. Next he tried to get one of his whale eyes as close to the box as possible, to get a really close look. That was tricky, with the shape a whale is, and it didn't make Wilber any wiser when he's finished his whale manoeuvres (it did give him a pain in the back).

All in all it seemed a pretty useless box, from a whale's point of view. Or at least from any point of view that Wilber could think of. Maybe you could talk to God through the box? Wilber tried the song of the humpback whale, but the box didn't answer. Then why were the clumsy creatures so excited? Maybe they were just stupid, not as smart as whales anyway. Down here at the bottom of the ocean it just seemed futile, all this fuss about a silly little box. Wilber was getting angry about this box, it bothered him that those clumsy creatures just might have thought of some idea that escaped him. In fact, the more he thought about it, the more he HATED that box. Save the whale!

After a while Wilber did try to calm down and be reasonable about the box. It was only a little box after all, nothing to get excited about. He could have just gone away and left the box to the eels, of course, but somehow that would have been a defeat.

Whales hate to say die, you know that, and Wilber was brave even among whales, the bravest whale in that patch of ocean, so he told himself often. Now you may think that Wilber wasn't too smart, even if he was brave, but honestly what use is a treasure of gold to a whale?

That was Wilber's problem. And I'm not sure you would have had a smarter idea than came to him, desperate and frustrated as he became. Have done with the box once and for all, leave no trace of it for any other creature, EAT it. Now that may not seem like a good idea to you, with all you know about skimming plankton and the sieves in a whale's gullet (or wherever those sieves are). The box would have stuck in his throat. So you may say. But where is a whale's throat? And what about Jonah anyway, how did he make his way into a whale's tummy (or out for that matter)? I'll give you a little time to answer those questions.

Not so smart are you? Now to be honest Wilber didn't know any better than you how a whale should eat a wooden box. He'd never tried such a thing before, why should he have? Well OK, but he was cross now and so he just attacked the box like it was his worst undersea enemy. He hit it a mighty blow with his tail, he sat on it with all his weight, bouncing up and down, he rammed it several times with his massive forehead, then the grabbed it by the side with his mouth and set off straight for the surface.

What next?
Wilber's frustration with that box full of treasure leads him to discover all sorts of things about the overwater world. As dad put it, 'his curiosity told him to wait and watch' something that dad was very skilled at. It was a pleasure to type out these stories because it's like having an old, familiar conversation with dad, and prompts you to think.